MICHIGAN'S BEST
Nature Centers and
Wilderness Preserves

Matt Forster

Adventure Publications
Cambridge, Minnesota

917.74
FOR
448-8386

Cover and book design by Jonathan Norberg

Edited by Brett Ortler

Photo credits:

Cover photos: All acquired via Shutterstock, with the exception of the sign post, courtesy of Matt Forster

All photos by Matt Forster unless noted

The following photos are copyright of their respective photographers. **Shutterstock:** 11, 76, 105/109, 105/111, 119, 120, 114/121, 125, 126 **Meridian Township:** 54 **Raven Hill Discovery Center:** 98, 99 **Stairway Down to Heaven ©** **Jimflix! on Flickr:** 90 **Scott Shields:** 100 **Todd Petersen:** 107 **Jacob Emerick blog. jacobemerick.com:** 118, 119 **Michael Huft:** 127 **Charles Eshbach:** 128 **Marilyn Keigley:** 129

10 9 8 7 6 5 4 3 2 1

Copyright 2017 by Matt Forster
Published by Adventure Publications
An imprint of AdventureKEEN
820 Cleveland Street South
Cambridge, Minnesota 55008
(800) 678-7006
www.adventurepublications.net
All rights reserved
Printed in U.S.A.
ISBN: 978-1-59193-680-0 eISBN: 978-1-59193-681-7

Table of Contents

Introduction

I didn't come to fully appreciate nature centers until my wife and I had kids. There's something about kids and nature. It's like kids and mac 'n' cheese, or kids and playgrounds. They go together. It's not always like that for adults, sadly. One day we find that we've spent a decade or two in classrooms or offices or in traffic, and all that time we spent outdoors as children seems a lifetime ago. So several years ago, as newly minted parents with a son and a daughter in hand, my wife and I began looking for different ways to learn about nature and spend some time outdoors.

Let me just say that if you enjoy nature centers, land conservancies, and preserves, Michigan is a great place to live. Our searches have been fruitful beyond our expectations. There are so many good people working behind the scenes, running organizations, donating land, and volunteering their time so that people will have opportunities to enjoy this state's natural beauty today and for generations to come.

Preserving something for the future is a theme that is echoed over and over in the mission statements and literature from nature-oriented organizations across the state. They are seeking to conserve forests and wetlands, bogs and fens, meadows and prairies, as well as historic farming practices, local culture, and the traditions of American Indian life.

While trying to capture what makes each of these sites worth visiting, I was often stymied by the inadequacy of words to describe the experience. Walking along one trail in west Michigan, I stopped for a moment and was overwhelmed by the sounds around me. Leaves sighing in the wind, birds fluttering in the underbrush, the trickle of water, frogs, cicadas, birdsong.

Then there are the smells. A cedar swamp smells sweeter than you might imagine. Tramping around a field of fragrant wildflowers, there's the unexpected bitter tang of broken stems. On a humid day, you might suddenly smell iron in the air and feel the cold, dry breeze that warns of a storm coming.

Yet none of these is a constant. A better writer could describe these locations so that you would feel like you have breathed the very air, but in the end, that person's experience would not be your experience. It keeps on changing, day to day, season to season.

As I traveled around researching sites for this project, a couple patterns emerged. Because these patterns necessarily affected what I included in this book, I want to share my observations.

By and large, nature centers cluster on the border between town and country, areas where there are plenty of people nearby who feel they don't have regular encounters with the natural world. After all, large populations are needed if a nonprofit organization is going to succeed. So though it almost seems ironic, most of the state's nature centers are within driving distance of the state's larger population centers.

In the more rural regions of the state, nature is preserved and conserved without a lot of the bells and whistles. Land conservancy groups can purchase land cheaper, when it's farther from town, and they don't need a large group of volunteers and donors to maintain and manage a property once it's been acquired.

I expected, for example, to find nature centers all over the Upper Peninsula, but, frankly, they're just not there. There are thousands of acres of wildlife and nature preserves, parks for outdoor recreation, and even some outdoor education opportunities, but nature centers, as we've come to understand them, are absent. Near metropolitan Detroit, where someone might understandably not expect to find many nature centers, there are more than a dozen.

There are some notable omissions in the book that deserve a mention, if only here in the introduction. These are Michigan's national parks. In the nomenclature of the National Park Service, Michigan has only one national *park*, **Isle Royale** in Lake Superior. The Great Lake State also has, appropriately enough, two national lakeshores, **Sleeping Bear Dunes** and **Pictured Rocks**. An entire book could be written about the natural beauty preserved in these three parks. Each has a visitor center that in some way explains its unique natural attractions.

In addition to its eponymous dunes, **Sleeping Bear Dunes National Lakeshore** offers a scenic drive through rolling, wooded dunes with panoramic views of the park and the lake. There is an early twentieth-century life-saving station—now a maritime museum—on site, as well as the historic buildings of Glen Haven, a former village site. The park also features two of the finest campgrounds on Lake Michigan.

Pictured Rocks National Lakeshore offers a different geological experience than its neighbor in the south. In contrast to Sleeping Bear's warm sand dunes, Pictured Rocks features bright sandstone cliffs overlooking Lake Superior. All told, there are 15 miles of cliffs, which tower 50 to 200 feet over the water. Visitors either find a motel in Grand Marais or Munising, or they set up camp in one of the park's campgrounds. To see the cliffs you can hike out to the bluffs or buy tickets for the tour boat that docks in Munising. There are a couple of waterfalls in the park that are also worth a visit.

It's not for nothing that **Isle Royale** is often included on the annual lists of "the most remote national parks." If you've ever driven 10 hours to the U.P.'s Keweenaw Peninsula only to jump on the ferry for the 3-hour trip across Lake Superior to the island, you know what I am talking about. Though you could make a day trip out of Isle Royale, the boat ride there and back makes it a long one. There's a lodge on site for overnight visits, but most people come for the incredible backpacking, the chance to see moose, beaver, and maybe even wolves, and the best wilderness camping in the Midwest.

If you visit every preserve or nature center in this book, you will find that not all of them are created equal. Some have been underfunded for many years, with facilities that need a little TLC. Others have benefited from a handful of amazing donors or an incredibly active corps of volunteers. All of these properties, however, have something to offer the public—the closer you look, the clearer the value of each place becomes.

And if you come across a place that you think could use some work, take it as a sign, roll up your sleeves, and join the fray.

As always, I hope you enjoy these nature centers and preserves, and maybe I'll see you out there!

Hours and Fees

Most, if not all, of the sites in this book are labors of love, and they are often run by volunteers and charitable organizations. Most require a nominal fee, which I've included with each account. Some of the sites in the book are part of Michigan's State Park system; to enter them, you'll need a Michigan State Recreation Passport, an annual vehicle pass that gives you access to all of the state parks in the system for just $11. (Nonresidents are charged $31.) For specifics, and all the benefits of the program, visit: www.michigan.gov/dnr/

Many of the sites in the book have hours that vary seasonally, and I've done the best I can to list them here. Hours and schedules change, however, so when in doubt, check the website or give them a call before you head out.

Visits by Theme

Not every visitor to a nature center or wilderness preserve visits for the same reason. Some come just for a short nature walk to unwind; others want to go hiking, to bird-watch or observe wildlife, or help the kids burn off some energy. Whatever your goal is, Michigan's nature center, and preserves have you covered. The following lists cover a variety of specific interests and should hopefully point you in the right direction.

Ten Best Places for a Short Nature Walk

5 Kensington Metropark Nature Center, pg. 25

14 Dahlem Environmental Education Center, pg. 43

17 Seven Ponds Nature Center, pg. 49

25 Fernwood Botanical Garden and Nature Preserve, pg. 65

27 Sarett Nature Center, pg. 69

32 Blandford Nature Center, pg. 79

34 Chippewa Nature Center, pg. 83

39 Grass River Natural Area, pg. 95

40 Hartwick Pines State Park, pg. 97

43 Elizabeth Kennedy Nature Center and the Thorne Swift Nature Preserve, pg. 103

Ten Best Places to Find Longer Nature Walks

10 Stony Creek Metropark Nature Center, pg. 35

11 Wint Nature Center at Independence Oaks, pg. 37

15 Eddy Discovery Center, pg. 45

16 For-Mar Nature Preserve and Arboretum, pg. 47

26 Warren Woods Natural Area, pg. 67

30 Nature Education Center at Hemlock Crossing Park, pg. 75

37 Green Point Dunes Nature Preserve, pg. 91

44 Marquette Island Preserves, pg. 107

49 Echo Lake Nature Preserve, pg. 119

53 Nara Nature Park and Nara Chalet Interpretive Center, pg. 127

Five Best Places for Tree Huggers

13 Hidden Lake Gardens, pg. 41

26 Warren Woods Natural Area, pg. 67

40 Hartwick Pines State Park, pg. 97

50 Sylvania Wilderness and Recreation Area, pg. 121

54 Estivant Pines Wilderness Nature Sanctuary, pg. 129

Five Best Places for Garden Lovers

Ten Best Places to Explore Wetlands

The Seven Geological Wonders (on Our List)

Ten Nature Sites that Kids Will Find Particularly Engaging

Five Best Places to Find Wildflowers

Ten Best Properties for Bird-Watching

Five Places with Captive Birds or Mounted Bird Collections

Southern Lower Peninsula

1. Marshlands Museum and Nature Center at Lake Erie Metropark
2. Crosswinds Marsh Wetland Interpretive Preserve
3. Oakwoods Metropark Nature Center
4. Leslie Science & Nature Center/ Black Pond Woods Nature Area
5. Kensington Metropark Nature Center
6. Farmington Hills Nature Center at Heritage Park
7. Red Oaks Nature Center
8. Lake St. Clair Metropark
9. Burgess-Shadbush Nature Center
10. Stony Creek Metropark Nature Center
11. Wint Nature Center at Independence Oaks
12. Environmental Discovery Center at Indian Springs Metropark
13. Hidden Lake Gardens
14. Dahlem Environmental Education Center
15. Eddy Discovery Center
16. For-Mar Nature Preserve and Arboretum
17. Seven Ponds Nature Center
18. Pine River Nature Center
19. DeVries Nature Conservancy
20. Harris Nature Center
21. Fenner Nature Center
22. Woldumar Nature Center
23. Kalamazoo Nature Center
24. Love Creek Nature Center
25. Fernwood Botanical Garden and Nature Preserve
26. Warren Woods Natural Area
27. Sarett Nature Center
28. Outdoor Discovery Center/ Macatawa Greenway
29. Degraaf Nature Center
30. Nature Education Center at Hemlock Crossing Park
31. Gillette Sand Dune Visitor Center at Hoffmaster State Park
32. Blandford Nature Center
33. Howard Christensen Nature Center
34. Chippewa Nature Center
35. Huron County Nature Center & Wilderness Arboretum

Northern Lower Peninsula

36. Johnson Hunting and Fishing Center at William Mitchell State Park
37. Green Point Dunes Nature Preserve
38. Boardman River Nature Center
39. Grass River Natural Area
40. Hartwick Pines State Park
41. Raven Hill Discovery Center
42. Sinkholes Pathway
43. Elizabeth Kennedy Nature Center and the Thorne Swift Nature Preserve

Northern Upper Peninsula

44. Marquette Island Preserves
45. Whitefish Point Bird Observatory
46. Tahquamenon Falls State Park
47. Seney National Wildlife Refuge

Western Upper Peninsula

48. MooseWood Nature Center
49. Echo Lake Nature Preserve
50. Sylvania Wilderness and Recreation Area
51. Kitch-iti-kipi at Palms Book State Park
52. Black River Scenic Byway Waterfalls
53. Nara Nature Park and Nara Chalet Interpretive Center
54. Estivant Pines Wilderness Nature Sanctuary

Southern Lower Peninsula

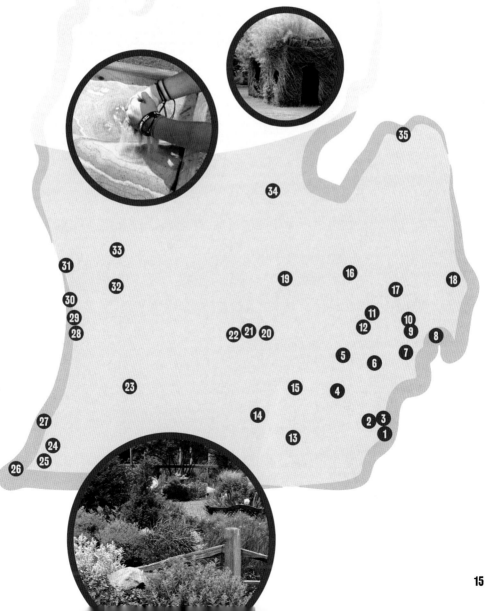

Marshlands Museum and Nature Center at Lake Erie Metropark

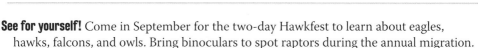

SAT.–SUN., 10–5; MUSEUM AND NATURE CENTER; FREE
METROPARK VEHICLE PERMIT REQUIRED: $10/DAY; $35/ANNUAL
32481 West Jefferson Avenue, Brownstown, MI 48173; (734) 379-5020
www.metroparks.com/Lake-Erie-Metropark-Marshlands-Museum-and-Nature-Center

See for yourself! Come in September for the two-day Hawkfest to learn about eagles, hawks, falcons, and owls. Bring binoculars to spot raptors during the annual migration.

The rundown:

The Lake Erie Metropark overlooks the mouth of the Detroit River. The park has a swimming pool with a water slide, a golf course, and a few other fun attractions. It is popular with cyclists and runners, and bird-watchers are also drawn to the park. In the spring and fall, thousands of birds migrate through the Great Lakes. Following the shorelines of Lake Huron, they are "funneled" into the St. Clair River and continue south. When the birds are moving, you will often find the northernmost parking lot full of cars and dozens of people with binoculars, necks craned toward the eastern sky.

The Marshlands Museum and Nature Center are both housed in the same building at the north end of the park. Duck hunting has a long history in this part of the state; in recent generations, duck hunters have proven to be some of Michigan's most avid conservationists. The museum chronicles the history of modern waterfowl hunting and includes antique decoys and exhibits about the sport over time. The Nature Center focuses on the ecology of the Great Lakes and boasts a 1,300-gallon aquarium featuring native fish.

Outside, there are a couple easy walks that originate in front of the Nature Center. The Trapper's Run loop, for example, follows the inside perimeter of a large hawthorn thicket. Four platforms close to the trail are intended as wetland overlooks. In the past, the invasive common reed (phragmites) has taken hold and blocked some of the views, but a few were still clear last time we visited. Another nice walk is the Cherry Island Trail loop, which follows the shore of Lake Erie for a bit and features the park's lotus beds. The American lotus is threatened in Michigan. However, you can find a vibrant patch of this aquatic flower by following the park's Cherry Island Trail from the boat launch area to the south. To see the lotus in bloom, time your visit carefully. The flower lasts only a couple days before the petals fall off.

It's a fact! Migrating birds follow the same routes from year to year, generation to generation. These paths are called flyways. The Atlantic and Mississippi flyways overlap in this part of Michigan, so the birds you see could be heading to the Gulf Coast or the Bahamas.

Crosswinds Marsh Wetland Interpretive Preserve

OPEN YEAR-ROUND, FROM DAWN TO DUSK
PROGRAMS OFFERED SEASONALLY; FREE
27600 Haggerty Road, New Boston, MI 48164; (734) 654-1223
www.waynecounty.com/dps/2019.htm

See for yourself! You can walk on water at Crosswinds Marsh—or over it at least—as there are 1.4 miles of boardwalk trails. The paths take you out onto the open marsh where keen eyes will catch the flickering outlines of fish just over the rail and spot stoic herons sunning themselves against a backdrop of native grasses.

The rundown:

When the first surveyors came to the parcel of land on the northwest corner of Haggerty Road and Oakville Waltz Road in what is now New Boston, they found a large complex of wet prairie and marshland. Later, at the end of the nineteenth century, settlers came flooding in from the east and most of the area's wetlands were drained and converted to farmland. This parcel was no exception. Then a decision was made 12 miles to the northeast that would change it back.

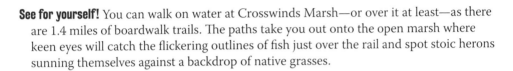

In 1994, the powers that be decided that Detroit Metropolitan Airport needed to expand the airport runway. The project destroyed acres of wetland, and state law requires that for every acre of wetland destroyed, 1.5 acres must be saved, or created. So the airport authorities purchased 1,000 acres of farmland on Haggerty Road in New Boston and began systematically flooding it. Native marsh plants were introduced, and when the project was complete, it was one of the world's largest man-made reconstructed marshes.

The marsh is now an interpretive preserve and operates as a Wayne County park. The boardwalks really set this place apart. All tallied, they account for about 1.4 miles of the preserve's trail system. Ducks, Canada geese, herons, and sandhill cranes float, stand, and roam nearby at their leisure. It's like taking a canoe out on the water without actually doing any of the work.

The boardwalk trails are certainly what makes the site special, but the marsh is also surrounded by dry meadows and forest that are crisscrossed by an extensive network of trails, which makes it a nice preserve for bird-watching, horseback riding (on designated paths), and hiking. A serious walker can choose loops from half a mile to 4.5 miles, and by combining loops you could make that even longer. The boardwalks are stroller friendly and good for those with disabilities.

It's a fact! More than 240 species of birds have been spotted at Crosswinds Marsh, including the endangered red knot, which migrates annually between the northern tundra of Canada to the most southern tip of South America.

Oakwoods Metropark Nature Center

PARK OPEN DAILY, 8–DUSK;
NATURE CENTER OPEN WEEKDAYS, 1–5; WEEKENDS, 10–5; FREE
METROPARK VEHICLE PERMIT REQUIRED: $10/DAY; $35/ANNUAL
32911 Willow Road, Flat Rock, MI 48134; (734) 782-3956
www.metroparks.com/Oakwoods-Metropark-Nature-Center

See for yourself! From behind the nature center, there's a spectacular view of the Huron River, which meanders by as it passes through the park. It's also a great place to launch a short out-and-back paddle trip on the park's canoe trail.

The rundown:

Oakwoods Metroparks is the third park in a chain that accounts for more than 4,500 continuous acres on 15 miles of the Huron River. (All three parks—Lower Huron, Willow, and Oakwood—are connected by a paved trail that continues 7 miles southeast to yet another park, the Lake Erie Metropark.) Of the three linked parks, Oakwoods is the least developed. There are equestrian trails and some nice picnic areas, but the real reason to head to Oakwoods is the nature center and its adjacent trails.

The nature center is the home of Hawkeye, a rescued red-tailed hawk that now lives on site. This guy is so popular that he has his own Facebook page. Though he shows up on the center's marketing pieces from time to time, his primary role is to teach visitors about raptors. Hawkeye lives in a large cage outside, so you can visit him almost anytime. Inside the nature center, there's a large 700-gallon turtle tank. Kids and adults can watch turtles in their simulated habitat and check out some of the center's other animal residents, including snakes, frogs, toads, and fish.

The nature center overlooks the Huron River, and the put-in for paddlers is just west of it. You can pick up a map for the Walk-in-Water Trail at the nature center; this out-and-back trip has you paddling for a half mile up the Huron River; the whole route is about a mile when you add in the return trip. Throughout the year, the park offers narrated tours in their 18-passenger voyageur canoe. If you can rustle up a dozen friends, there's a group rate for the tour in the 34-foot canoe.

The nature trails are also worth walking. With the exception of the Butterfly Trail, all of the trails begin right here at the center. There are four loops offering different experiences of the nearby woods and the river. For the Butterfly Trail, head over to the parking lot for the Cedar Knoll Picnic Area. This small loop is an official monarch butterfly way station and is certified by Monarch Watch, an organization dedicated to saving this threatened species.

It's a fact! The Huron River widens downstream because of a dam in Flat Rock. Once a gristmill, Henry Ford bought the dam to power a factory that built headlights.

Leslie Science & Nature Center
Black Pond Woods Nature Area

TRAILS OPEN DAILY, DAWN TO DUSK; OFFICE OPEN WEEKDAYS, 8–4; FREE
1831 Traver Road, Ann Arbor, MI 48105; (734) 997-1553
www.lesliesnc.org

See for yourself! Visit on the second Saturday of the month for raptor feeding sessions! Note: This isn't for the squeamish; the raptors are fed their natural diet of small mammals.

The rundown:

Just a stone's throw from downtown Ann Arbor, tucked under the arm of M-14 and surrounded by neighborhoods and a golf course, the very existence of the Black Pond Woods Nature Area comes as a pleasant surprise. Even with the proximity to all the urban hustle and bustle, the property is wonderfully secluded, and once you head into the woods, the world of strip malls and gas stations seems to fall away.

The Leslie Science and Nature Center was once the home of Dr. Eugene and Emily Leslie. They lived on the property from 1923 through 1976, planting trees and adding outbuildings over the years. Most of these buildings are used today. Their former honey house, in which they kept bees, is now the Critter House. The larger, newer building you will see when you visit is the DTE Energy Nature House, which is used for programs and events. Behind the main house is a collection of smaller structures. These are the birds of prey and raptor enclosures. The birds are housed outdoors so you can visit them whenever you stop by. There's a bald eagle, owls, and hawks, and you can get close enough that you will want to remember not to stick a finger behind the wire mesh.

Black Pond Woods extends north of the nature center. This is classic moraine terrain, the characteristic debris left behind by glaciers. Here, the forest rises and falls, making for steep climbing at times. The main trail is a mile in length and takes you back to Black Pond. Typical of the terrain, this is a kettle pond; kettle ponds and lakes formed when a large piece of ice fell from a retreating glacier. It pushed into the ground, creating a basin, and when it later melted, it left this pond behind.

Geocachers will want to take note: The nature area has three geocaches hidden on the property, each highlighting one of the area's nature features. I imagine that some people will find this a great way to learn about the property, especially if there are kids involved.

Take special note: The public restrooms are not always open.

It's a fact! You might be asking, "Why would they cage birds at a nature center? Shouldn't birds live free?" Well, set your mind at rest. The raptors here have all suffered some kind of permanent injury that makes it impossible for them to survive in the wild.

Kensington Metropark Nature Center

MON., 1–5; TUE.–SUN., 10–5; NATURE CENTER FREE
METROPARK VEHICLE PERMIT REQUIRED: $10/DAY; $35/ANNUAL
Highridge Drive, Milford, MI 48380; (810) 227-8917
www.metroparks.com/Kensington-Metropark-Nature-Center

See for yourself! With a little birdseed in your palm, songbirds will happily alight upon your hand for a nibble. You will most likely find them when you walk the trail just west of the nature center; it runs due north and south.

The rundown:

Kensington is a sprawling park that follows a long swath of the Huron River, including the large Kent Lake. It is one of the most popular parks in the Metropark system. Recreation opportunities abound, and it's no wonder that 2.5 million visitors come each year to ride their bikes, jog, rollerblade, or play in the water. Thankfully, the Nature Center has been set aside as an area specifically dedicated for hiking; no biking or running are allowed there.

The Nature Center at Kensington Metropark was once a family's summer retreat. Jo Labadie was a labor leader and wanted to create a place where workers could escape during the summer months. Later, Jo's children donated the property to the county to be used as a park.

The Nature Center overlooks Kingfisher Lagoon. Nearby Wildwing Lake is connected to the lagoon by a marsh. Perfectly situated nature trails radiate out from the center and take you through wetlands or up into dry woodlands. All told, there are 6 miles of nature trails, but several include loops that are short enough to be hiked in 15 minutes.

Casual bird-watchers will appreciate the sandhill cranes that wander around the Nature Center building during the summer. You're likely to encounter other birds as well; several of the nature paths are lined by dense vegetation, and numerous times we've rounded a corner to see a couple of children with small songbirds eating from their hands. I suspect the leaves are thick enough for birds to hide and the trails wide enough for them to feel comfortable. So bring some birdseed in your pocket, in case the opportunity arises.

The Nature Center building exhibits a few live animals and has a couple of games for the kids, but the real attraction here is getting outside, taking a walk, and seeing some birds. There are binoculars for looking out over the lagoon, and all along the trails you will see signs identifying trees and other natural features. The Nature Center is located in the southwestern half of the park.

It's a fact! The sandhill cranes that pass through Nebraska's Sandhills may be coming from as far north as Siberia on their way to Mexico. Those in Michigan come from much closer—north of Lake Huron in Ontario—and end up in Florida.

Please
Do Not
Touch
Display

Farmington Hills Nature Center at Heritage Park

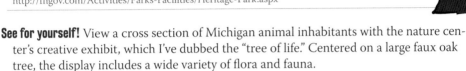

SUN., NOON–5; MON.–SAT., 10–5. CLOSED MONDAYS, DEC.–MAR.; FREE
24915 Farmington Road, Farmington Hills, MI 48336; (248) 477-1135
http://fhgov.com/Activities/Parks-Facilities/Heritage-Park.aspx

See for yourself! View a cross section of Michigan animal inhabitants with the nature center's creative exhibit, which I've dubbed the "tree of life." Centered on a large faux oak tree, the display includes a wide variety of flora and fauna.

The rundown:

Municipal parks are common enough in the 'burbs, but few are as expansive as Heritage Park in Farmington Hills. For years, Farmington Hills was a small farming village outside of Detroit. As the metro area grew, and land was turned over to build subdivisions, the Spicer family kept on farming, all the way into the 1980s. Farmington Hills bought the farm in 1985 and Heritage Park was born.

The park's 211 acres border Farmington Road between 10 Mile Road and 11 Mile Road. The Upper Rouge River passes through the west half of the property, and 4.5 miles of trails wind through the park. Close to the park entrance there are a number of historic buildings, including the Gray-Spicer House, a barn, and a stable. Separated from the splash pad and concessions area, the Farmington Hills Nature Center is tucked into a quiet corner of the park, next to the Spicer House.

The nature center features great wildlife exhibits. The centerpiece is the large oak tree surrounded by wildlife habitat. There are also aquariums, a touch table, and other hands-on interactive exhibits. The paved Estate Trail is a half mile long and leaves from the nature center, looping around a bluebird nesting area. Along the way it passes a playground and the park's Serenity Garden.

Every year, the park hosts a number of classes, day camps, and events. One of the annual events is the Great Farmington Hills Campout. Aimed at encouraging families to camp, this overnight event brings both beginning and seasoned campers together for a day of activities and a night of sleeping in a tent.

It's a fact! Parks in Michigan are all fighting the garlic mustard invasion these days. Not only does the plant push out native species, but it also changes the soil so that other plants simply won't grow. Is there a bright side? Kind of: The plant was brought to North America by settlers for use as a garden herb, and its leaves can be used to make a delicious pesto.

Red Oaks Nature Center

SUN., NOON–5; TUE.–SAT., 10–5. OPEN UNTIL 8 ON SAT., MEMORIAL DAY–LABOR DAY
NATURE CENTER FREE; VEHICLE PERMIT REQUIRED FOR PARK
($5 PER DAY FOR COUNTY RESIDENTS/$12 PER DAY FOR NONRESIDENTS)
30300 Hales Street, Madison Heights, MI 48071; (248) 585-0100;
www.destinationoakland.com/parksandtrails/parks/RedOaks/Pages/NatureCenter.aspx

See for yourself! A 200-year-old oak, a butterfly garden, a forest of dead ash trees ravaged by emerald ash borers, and a meadow replete with wildflowers are found on the park's three interpretive nature trails. They make for a great walk, and with a guide map in hand, it's the perfect place to learn something new.

The rundown:

Red Oaks County Park is essentially a long corridor of green space that sits atop the Red Run drain. It was clearly designed for recreation. There is a nine-hole golf course, a water park, a soccer complex, and a dog park. The nature center sits off to the side. The park only recently took over management of the neighboring Madison Heights Nature Center in the Suarez Friendship Woods, rechristening it the Red Oaks Nature Center.

Urban areas sometimes hide the most surprising natural spaces. The Red Oaks Nature Center consists of 38 acres of forest tucked between two neighborhoods off of 13 Mile Road. The county park next door has 168 acres but far fewer trees. This is the George W. Suarez Friendship Woods, named for the longtime mayor of Madison Heights.

There are three natural trail loops here—the Forest Trail, the Sensory Trail, and the Habitat Trail. They add up to 1.3 miles of paved pathway. The Sensory Trail is the shortest of the lot and passes a wooded pond; the area has plenty of wildlife, from white-tailed deer to cotton-tail rabbits.

Inside the nature center, a tall wall of windows looks out over the woods. Constructed of logs and with a large field-stone fireplace, it has a definite lodge atmosphere. There are numerous exhibits—aquariums with live animals, an indoor pond, and displays that change with the season. Kids can take a closer look with the hands-on microscope, or put on their own puppet show.

It's a fact! Driving on Hale Street to the nature center, you will cross over Red Run, a tributary of the Clinton River. Unseen now, this buried creek once had fingers that spread as far west as Beaumont Hospital. It's now a covered drain, only seeing the light of day when it exits the tunnel at Dequindre Road, east of the Red Oaks water park.

Lake St. Clair Metropark

DURING SCHOOL SEASON, WEEKDAYS, 1–5; DAILY IN SUMMER, 10–5
NATURE CENTER FREE
METROPARK VEHICLE PERMIT REQUIRED: $10/DAY; $35/ANNUAL
31300 Metro Parkway, Harrison Township, MI 48045; (586) 463-4581;
www.metroparks.com

See for yourself! Take a tour of Lake St. Clair on one of the park's Discovery Cruises. Several hours on the water is enough to learn all about anything from weather and wildlife to shipwrecks and astronomy.

The rundown:

The Lake St. Clair Metropark is located just south of the mouth of the Clinton River. In the summer, most visitors come to the park for the 1,000-foot Metro Beach on Lake St. Clair (which is dwarfed by the expansive parking lot that's filled on sunny weekends). The park also has a North and South Marina for boaters, a beach shop, and even a launch area for kite surfing.

Tucked in the middle of the park, you will find the nature center, which has its own parking lot. The center explores the importance of the area's waterway and wetlands. The Clinton River is second only to the Huron River in terms of the area the watershed drains, 760 square miles in all, and it played a key role in American Indian transportation and early European exploration. The center teaches a little about that human history, as well, telling the story of the first European trappers and traders. In the summer, it's even home to a weekend-long Voyageur Encampment, complete with reenactors who set up camp at the park so visitors can learn about life in the Great Lakes before 1800.

While the nature center is itself worth a visit, the real attractions are outside. There are several trail routes, and all are a mile or less. The north and west sides of the park are marsh, and the trails take you to the edge. For a bird's-eye view, there's an observation deck looking out on the south marsh. The center also has a nice schedule of nature programs.

The park's Summer Discovery Cruises might be the most unique feature of the park for nature lovers. You can spend a lot of time in Michigan looking out at water; these cruises take you out on the water. Some of the cruises explore Great Lakes shipping. Others take visitors out and tell the stories of area shipwrecks or examine the history of Lake St. Clair. There are also a number of cruises dedicated to helping passengers understand the natural ecosystem of this little corner of the world.

It's a fact! Lake St. Clair has an average depth of 11 feet. In order for ships to pass through the lake, Canada and the United States have to maintain a shipping channel that's 27 feet deep.

9

Burgess-Shadbush Nature Center

SUN., NOON–5; WED.–SAT., 9:30–6; FREE
4101 River Bends Drive, Utica, MI 48317; (586) 323-2478
www.shelbytwp.org/burgess-shadbush_nature_center/index.html

See for yourself! The Shadbush Master Gardens are not to be missed—look for the section of historic plants and note the native species that might work in your own garden.

The rundown:

The Burgess-Shadbush Nature Center is located in River Bends Park on a section of the park preserved as the Shadbush Tract. The nature center is found less than 2 miles north of M-59, just east of Ryan Road, though the park follows the river southeast back to the highway.

The property has a fascinating history. A historic marker just east of the nature center tells the story of Spring Hill Farm. Established in the 1830s, the Lerich family used their property to help escaped slaves, marking their underground shelter with a large cedar tree, which became known as the "Beacon Tree." A hundred years later in 1939, the property was purchased by none other than Joe Louis, heavyweight champion of the world. He sold it five years later. From 1955 through 1974, it was part of a Nike missile defense system run by the US government. None of this history, aside from a historical marker, is evident on site today.

The first thing you notice when you visit the nature center is the cluster of gardens west of the building. Visitors who wander the mulch paths will find a deer-resistant garden, a pollinator garden, and a teaching garden. There are also historic plants and native species located here. The nature center staff is rightfully proud of their interactive Clinton River exhibit. This is a hands-on way for kids and adults to learn about the animals that call this river home. Kids can even climb through a riverbank tunnel where there are more interactive displays.

The Shadbush Tract accounts for 80 acres of the park. The site has been a nature study area since 1966. Once a flat river delta, the area was inundated by runoff from melting glaciers. This often-rocky debris helped form the steep hillsides in the area and gave the area its nickname, "the little Grand Canyon of Macomb County." The area is also home to a tamarack swamp; over the years, numerous wildlife inventories have been taken, documenting the incredible variety of flora and fauna present here. If you want to tour the tract, start out at the nature center and pick up the Shadbush Trail. From there, a long boardwalk traces a path through the wetlands north to the Clinton River.

It's a fact! Also known as the serviceberry, the shadbush is a member of the rose family and belongs to the genus Amelanchier; the shadbush gets its name because it blooms around the same time that shad (a type of fish) swim upriver to spawn in Michigan.

33

10

Stony Creek Metropark Nature Center

DURING SCHOOL SEASON MON.–FRI., 1–5; SAT.–SUN., 10–5
SUMMER DAILY, 10–5; NATURE CENTER FREE
METROPARK VEHICLE PERMIT REQUIRED: $10/DAY; $35/ANNUAL
4300 Main Park Road, Shelby Township, MI 48316; (586) 781-9113
www.metroparks.com/Stony-Creek-Metropark-Nature-Center

See for yourself! Short loops are great for some folks, but at Stony Creek, you can combine several of the popular loops and turn that quick jaunt in the woods into an 8-mile hike.

The rundown:

The Stony Creek Nature Center features a modest exhibit space as well as rooms for classes and other programs. The general exhibit area has live animals on display, including frogs, turtles, snakes, and fish. Several of the animal tanks are easily accessible for little kids, so they can get a close look without you having to lift them.

The Nature Center is also the central hub for the park's various nature programs. They have programs for school field trips and homeschoolers, as well as a lot of summer activities. One program takes guests out in a 34-foot voyageur canoe to learn about Stony Creek Lake.

Stony Creek is an important local waterway. It enters the park from the north and meanders 2 miles before it eventually widens into Stony Creek Lake. It passes through two dams and leaves the park to the south. The Nature Center is at the north end of the park and where you will also find all of the nature trails. At some point or other, all of the trails dally alongside the creek a bit, but aside from that common feature, they offer hikes through a variety of different habitats, including high oak savanna, forest, and glacial kettles (one dry and wooded, the other seasonally wet). All of these habitats are the result of the long retreat of the glaciers during the last ice age. Stony Creek's interpretive signs and programs do a good job of translating that history to show how this glacial impact led directly to the diverse animals and plant communities found at the park today.

When you're planning a walk at Stony Creek, take note of the Inwood Trails north of Inwood Road. This part of the park has its own parking area, and you can also get there by way of a short connector trail off the Nature Center's Habitat Trail. These routes are clearly marked on the park map, but they are not as busy as the rest of the park, and if you are looking for a solitary hike, they make a nice alternative.

It's a fact! Fire plays an important role in many habitats, as it controls undergrowth and stimulates new growth. In order to maintain the balance at Stony Creek, the park performs controlled burns. Invasive species are less resistant to fire, so these fires keep invasive species like autumn olive from spreading and allow native prairie grasses to thrive.

11

Wint Nature Center at Independence Oaks

NATURE CENTER OPEN FRI.–SAT., 10–5; SUN., 1–5; PARK OPEN DAILY DAWN TO DUSK
NATURE CENTER FREE; VEHICLE PERMIT REQUIRED FOR PARK
($5/DAY FOR OAKLAND COUNTY RESIDENTS; $12/DAY FOR NONRESIDENTS)
9501 Sashabaw Road, Clarkston, MI 48348; (248) 625-6473
www.destinationoakland.com/parksandtrails/wintnaturecenter

See for yourself! If a walk in the woods isn't your thing, the park rents boats in the summer for exploring Crooked Lake.

The rundown:

Independence Oaks continues to be one of my favorite places to hike in the Detroit metro area. Located just a few miles from downtown Clarkston, and about 40 miles from Detroit, it's home to more than 12 miles of trails that wind through 1,200 acres of rolling moraines and low washout plains. There are wetlands, lakes, shady forests, and sunny meadows. The paths themselves range from dirt paths for walking and cross-country skiing to paved trails for walking, rollerblading, and biking. There's also a beach for swimming, and you can go fishing in Crooked Lake.

The Wint Nature Center is found in the northwest corner of the park, just west of Crooked Lake. The center has rooms for meetings and various programs, as well as a number of excellent exhibits. On both sides of its indoor boardwalk, dioramas highlight the importance of wetlands and discuss the water cycle. Directly beneath your feet, fish are frozen in place. On one side of the walk, terrariums house various reptiles.

The main exhibits are engaging and geared toward children, with many hands-on displays. An interactive quiz, for example, teaches kids about different kinds of soil. There is also a stage prepped for a puppet show and a turkey cut-out for goofy photo-ops. And, of course, there are summer camps and a schedule full of nature activities.

With the exception of the paved River Trail, all of the park's trails pass by the nature center. Less than a mile long, the Habitat Trail makes a short loop behind the building. The path is wide and primarily composed of wood chips. The Rockridge Trail is twice as long and a bit more challenging; it follows the ridge of a moraine. At the southern end of the loop is an observation tower where several flights of stairs lead you to an exposed deck overlooking the woods. If hiking is your thing, be sure to check out the longer trails here—the Springhill Loop and the Lakeshore Loop. The latter makes an easy lap around Crooked Lake, while the former is the longest of the bunch (3.2 miles) and offers steep climbs through an airy forest.

It's a fact! Wetlands in this township form the headwaters of southeast Michigan's most important rivers—the Huron and Clinton Rivers.

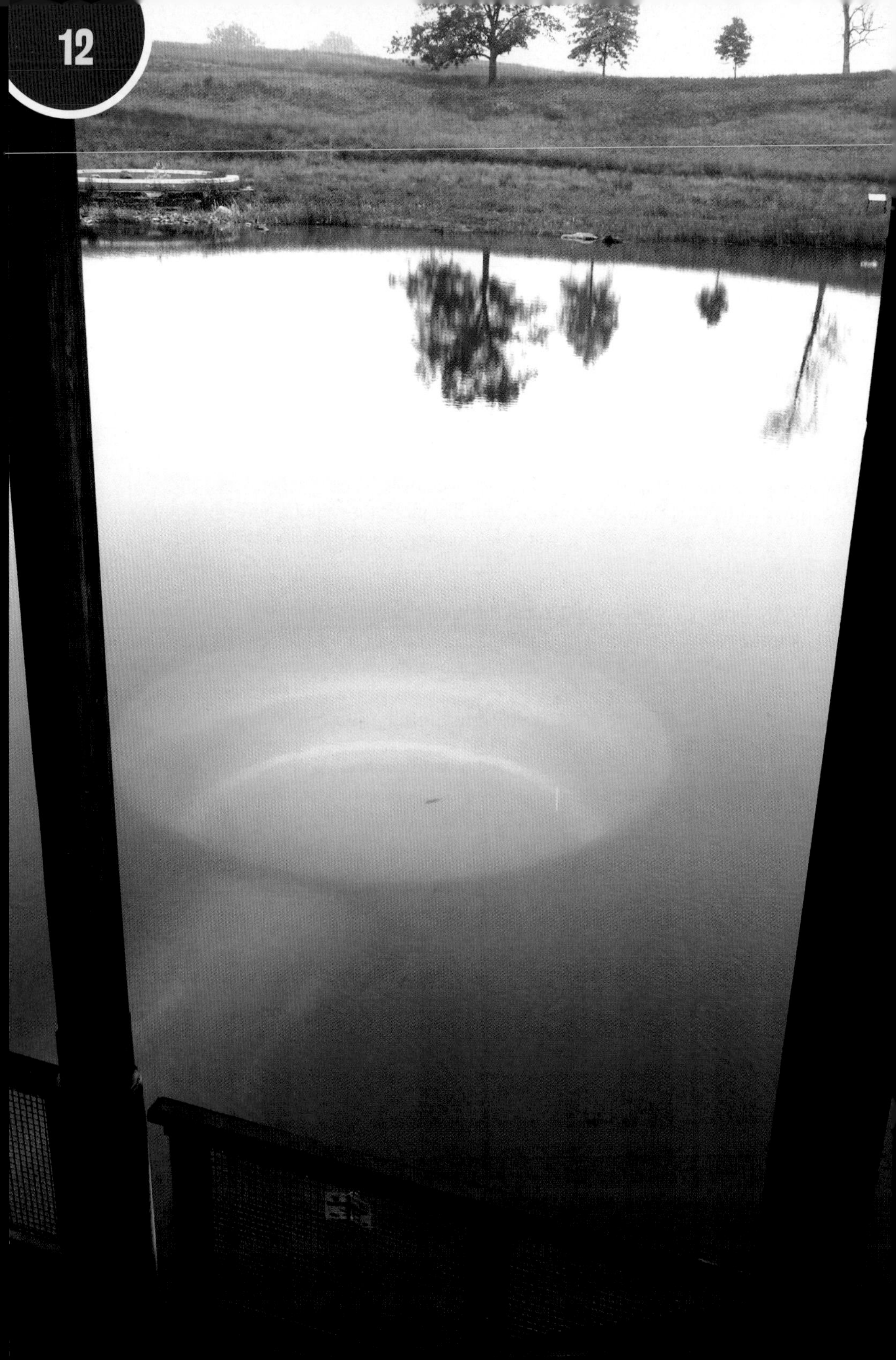

12

Environmental Discovery Center at Indian Springs Metropark

DAILY, 9–5; NATURE CENTER FREE
METROPARK VEHICLE PERMIT REQUIRED: $10/DAY; $35/ANNUAL
5200 Indian Trail, White Lake, MI 48386; (248) 625-6640
www.metroparks.com/indian-springs-metropark

See for yourself! The nature center at Indian Springs not only overlooks a small pond, it underlooks it too! Head to the basement to explore the underwater viewing dome.

The rundown:

The 2,500-acre Indian Springs Metropark is known for a couple things: a public golf course, an amazing splash pad, and the Environmental Discovery Center. The center is very popular with schoolkids on field trips, homeschool groups, and others who come to use the classrooms and lab facilities. There are some visually stunning displays here, but chances are, you're not visiting for the exhibits. Instead, you're going to want to head downstairs.

The center was built overlooking a pond. Decks on the upper level and lower level look out over the water, and around the pond, the path invites visitors to stop and observe what's going on near and in the pond. In the basement, there's a unique underwater observation room. The room is an arched tunnel that leads out to a clear dome under the pond. The water is sometimes murky green, but you can almost always see fish swimming by, and it's a great way to get a different perspective on pond life. It's much brighter below the water than you might imagine from standing on the shore.

Indian Springs is also located near the headwaters of the Huron River. From the road, Indian Springs Metropark seems to consist of open grassland with some groves of trees here and there, but the north section of the park is a wooded wetland called the Huron Swamp. It's not like Kermit the Frog's home in Georgia's Okefenokee Swamp, dripping with moss and inhabited by alligators. Instead, it's more of a soggy forest. A long path loops through the swamp, following high ground where it can and using boardwalks where it can't.

There's a pond at the far end of the loop. In the early spring, this swamp is alive with skunk cabbage. This early bloomer actually generates its own heat and melts its way through the snow in order to be the first plant of the season to catch the sunlight. Later in the spring, the ephemerals come out for their turn in the sun, and the walk is fantastic.

It's a fact! Michigan's only venomous snake, the eastern massasauga rattlesnake, lives in or near wetlands, but it's incredibly unlikely you'll encounter one, as the snake is threatened in the state and quite secretive and wary of people.

13

Hidden Lake Gardens

OPEN DAILY, 9–7, APRIL–OCT.; OPEN 9–4, NOV.–MAR.
$3 FOR EVERYONE AGE 3 AND OLDER
6214 Monroe Road, Tipton, MI 49287; (517) 431-2060
hiddenlakegardens.msu.edu

See for yourself! The bonsai collection at Hidden Lakes Gardens is the best around. This traditional art form involves working with nature to create something new, yet familiar.

The rundown:

This 755-acre botanical garden and arboretum is managed by Michigan State University. Located 8 miles west of Tecumseh in a part of the state known as the Irish Hills, this sprawling site began as a retired businessman's pet project. In 1926, Howard Fee bought 200 acres around the Hidden Lake and began growing nursery plants, eventually creating picturesque gardens. As his gardens grew, he decided to build a road so people could drive through and see them. After working on the project for a couple of decades, he gave the property to the university to preserve it for the public.

Glaciers created the unique rolling terrain found at Hidden Lake Gardens. These hills were created because the area was situated between two lobes of a glacier. Throughout the property you find kettle holes and kames (irregular hills left behind by glaciers melting). Hidden Lake itself is a kettle lake, another product of the state's glacial history.

As you might expect, this place is a gardener's delight. Many green thumbs spend hours here, driving the roads, walking the paths, and exploring the exquisite gardens. Next to Hidden Lake is a large Visitor Center, and just to the west of that is the Conservatory. The Conservatory features three different environments—arid, temperate, and tropical—allowing the staff to grow plants from around the world. Gardens are found both here and throughout the property.

There are three collections especially worth noting. The first is the Hosta Hillside. This collection of hostas includes 800 varieties of the Michigan landscaper's staple. The hillside overlooks Hidden Lake, and visitors enjoy the shady location as much as the plants do. Another exhibit not to miss is the bonsai collection. Most of these trees were donated to the gardens, and many are very mature. Every September, there's a special bonsai event that enthusiasts will not want to miss. Finally, keep an eye out for the gardens' dwarf and rare conifers. This collection consists of 500 trees in all, and they are planted throughout the property.

It's a fact! During the ice age, this area was located between two lobes of a glacier. To the west was the Saginaw Lobe, and to the east the Huron-Erie Lobe. They were part of the Laurentide Ice Sheet, which retreated about 20,000 years ago.

14

NATALIE EMMONS
MEMORIAL CHILDREN'S GARDEN

"LET CHILDREN WALK WITH NATURE, LET THEM SEE THE BEAUTIFUL BLENDINGS
AND COMMUNIONS OF DEATH AND LIFE, THEIR JOYOUS INSEPARABLE UNITY,
AS TAUGHT IN WOODS AND MEADOWS, PLAINS AND MOUNTAINS AND STREAMS
OF OUR BLESSED STAR, AND THEY WILL LEARN THAT DEATH IS STINGLESS INDEED,
AND AS BEAUTIFUL AS LIFE." JOHN MUIR

DONATED BY LOVING FRIENDS AND FAMILY OF
NATALIE HAGUE EMMONS

Dahlem Environmental Education Center

NATURE CENTER BUILDING SUN., 12–5; TUE.–FRI., 9–5; SAT., 10–5;
TRAILS OPEN DAWN TO DUSK; FREE
7117 South Jackson Road, Jackson, MI 49201; (517) 782-3453;
www.dahlemcenter.org

See for yourself! The Nature for All Trail at the Dahlem Environmental Education Center is a 3/8-mile nature walk. The path has a hard-packed surface, making it perfect for wheelchairs, strollers, walkers, and wagons.

The rundown:

The Dahlem Environmental Education Center traces its history to the early 1960s when Jackson Junior College received a gift of 270 acres of land and some farm buildings. Later, seeing an opportunity, the school's biology department decided to use the property for a nature center. In 1974, the college purchased the adjacent Fannie Beach Arboretum and increased the size of the center to nearly 300 acres.

Today, the Jackson Junior College is now called Jackson College, the farm buildings are the Dahlem Ecology Farm, and the arboretum is the site of the center's administrative and interpretive headquarters. From the main entrance on South Jackson Road, you will find offices, classrooms, a small exhibit space, and a gift shop.

Around the arboretum, and closer to the buildings, there are a number of gardens, including the Children's Garden, the Geology Garden, and the Sensory Garden. There is also the Nature Playscape, which encourages unstructured playtime. The signature trail here is the hard-packed Nature for All Trail, which is under half a mile and accessible for everyone. It begins at the Children's Garden and makes an elongated loop out to Crouch Creek and back again.

There are two clusters of trails at the center. The first group makes smaller loops through the arboretum. These trails all begin in the parking lot. One of these is the Arboretum Trail, which leads back to a bridge that crosses Crouch Creek and into a much larger section of the property. Between Wickwire and East Kimmel Roads, you'll find the site's second group of trails, and they wind through a variety of ecosystems, including a black oak savanna, an oak-hickory forest, as well as native prairie, wet meadows, a pond, and a fen. The center offers year-round educational programs for student groups and families, and it also hosts the annual Birds, Blooms, and Butterflies Festival.

It's a fact! According to the Audubon Society, over the past couple of decades bluebird boxes have helped populations of eastern, western, and mountain bluebirds recover from the freefall they'd been in during the middle part of the twentieth century.

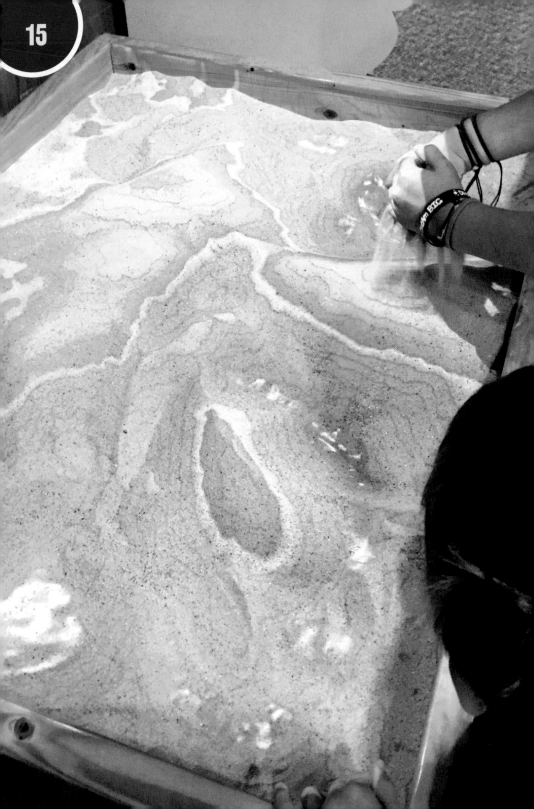

15

Eddy Discovery Center

SUMMER SUN., 12–5; MON.–SAT., 10–5; CLOSED MON. IN SHOULDER SEASONS
JAN.–MAR. OPEN WEEKENDS ONLY
MICHIGAN RECREATION PASSPORT REQUIRED (PAGE 7)
Green Point Road, Frankfort, MI 49635; (231) 929-7911
www.gtrlc.org/recreation-events/preserve/green-point-dunes-nature-preserve

See for yourself! We have carnivorous plants in Michigan; you can see them on the Discovery Center's bog trail, which is home to pitcher plants, bladderworts, and sundews.

The rundown:

At 21,000 acres, Waterloo State Recreation Area is the largest park in Michigan's Lower Peninsula. There are campgrounds, beaches, boat launches, and trails. On the park's east side, a short drive from Chelsea, is the Eddy Discovery Center. The center sits in a designated natural area surrounded by small lakes and wetlands, where it serves as a hub of sorts for a network of interpretive nature trails.

The newly renovated exhibit hall features a large interactive map of the area. A variety of ecosystems are a short walk from the center and they include a beech-maple forest, a hardwood swamp, and a bog; the hall's exhibits give visitors the lowdown on what they'll see when heading out into the park. Before European settlement, this area was a much different place. Inhabited since the time of the Paleo-Indian thousands of years ago, spear points, a dugout canoe, and other artifacts have been found here. The center's geology room goes back even further in history and explores the ice age with a walk-in model ice cave; other exhibits look back to the age of fossils.

The Waterloo-Pinckney Trail is the only backpacking trail in southeast Michigan, and 23 miles of the trail cross the Waterloo Recreation Area before continuing into the adjacent Pinckney Recreation Area. The route in the park dips south and around Mill Lake and passes right by the Discovery Center.

When visitors decide to hike the Oak Woods Trail and the Lakeview Trail—two of the center's nature loops—they are piggy-backing on the Waterloo-Pinckney Trail for a short bit. These two loops offer views of Mill Lake. Closer to the nature center, there's also a paved accessible path. For visitors with a yen to walk, the Waterloo-Pinckney Trail continues on to the north and west. The trail offers some steep climbs, especially the hike up to the overlook behind the ranger station on McClure Road, but there is some beautiful scenery along the way, concluding with a view of Crooked Lake. The trek out is a little more than 2 miles. It's not a loop, so be prepared to walk both ways or arrange a ride.

It's a fact! In 1931, there were only 17 pairs of sandhill cranes left in the Lower Peninsula, and fewer than 100 pairs in the Upper Peninsula. The population has rebounded since then, and today experts put the population at more than 20,000.

16

For-Mar Nature Preserve and Arboretum

VISITOR CENTER DAILY, 8–5; TRAILS DAILY, 8–SUNSET; FREE
2142 North Genesee Road, Burton, MI 48509; (810) 736-7100;
www.geneseecountyparks.org/pages/formar

See for yourself! The Foote Bird Museum has more than 600 mounted birds in its collection. It's only open a couple of hours on Sunday, though, so plan accordingly.

The rundown:

A 383-acre preserve located east of Flint in Genesee County, the For-Mar Nature Preserve and Arboretum is located just a short drive from the city. It's an impressive park. There are 7 miles of hiking trails amid the rolling hills, mature forests, wetlands, ponds, and open meadows. In the summer, you will always find families out hiking the trails. The most recent addition to the preserve is an expansive tree house. Accessible to visitors with disabilities, the tree house isn't just a fun play area. It also serves as classroom space, taking the pressure off the visitor center, which has been operating at capacity for some years now.

Your visit begins at the visitor center, where there are wildlife displays and a number of hands-on exhibits. The center's backpack program is pretty popular and does a good job of enhancing the outdoor experience. Before heading out on the trails, pick up a discovery backpack. There are five different packs to suit your interests. The Active Living pack, for example, includes a jump rope, yoga guide, and hand weights. The Basic Birding pack has binoculars for kids and an electric birdsong identifier.

Kearsley Creek is another integral part of the park. It's a significant tributary of the Flint River; by the time it reaches For-Mar, it has grown into a decent-size stream. It flows through the property south-to-north, and three bridges keep the footpaths on both sides of the creek connected. Some of the preserve's best trails track closely with the curves of the creek. In these woods you will find wetlands and several ponds with some unique additions. For example, the Ground Water Pond, close to the visitor center, has an observation tower that gives you a vantage point above the dense vegetation that surrounds the pond. The Runoff Pond has a windmill. Remember, when walking the trails, running and biking are only allowed on the gravel service drive, and pets are not allowed.

If you come on a Sunday, between 2 and 4 o'clock, be sure to shuffle over to the Foote Bird Museum. It's located in the DeWaters Education Center. The museum collection features more than 600 mounted birds as well as bird eggs. The visitor center also offers classes and programs, which run the gamut. You could find yourself a cooking class or learn how to start beekeeping. There's also a robust program of community gardening.

It's a fact! The new tree house at For-Mar was built by Nelson Treehouse and Supply and is featured on the Animal Planet show, *Treehouse Masters*.

17

Seven Ponds Nature Center

NATURE CENTER TUE.–SUN., 9–5; GROUNDS DAWN TO DUSK;
ADULTS $3, CHILDREN FREE
3854 Crawford Road, Dryden, MI 48428; (810) 796-3200;
www.sevenponds.org

See for yourself! The center's collection of Michigan birds includes more than 150 specimens, including everything from waterfowl and raptors to songbirds. The most unique of the bunch might just be the passenger pigeon, which went extinct more than 100 years ago.

The rundown:

The Seven Ponds Nature Center is located east of Metamora. This is Michigan's horse country. Wander off the main road and you're bound to find rolling green fields lined with pristine white fences. Drive down Caulkins Road, however, and the landscape grows a bit more natural. Fields give way to forests, cedar swamps, and ponds.

The nature center features 468 acres, 7 glacial lakes, and 8 miles of trails that traverse the property. Examples include Paul's Woods Trail in the southern part of the preserve and the North-80 Trail, with its fields and forests.

The Interpretive Building is located at the heart of Seven Ponds. This is where you begin your visit (and pay your fees). The building's main exhibit hall has many different specimens of local wildlife, including 150-plus native Michigan birds. It also has a touch table, where you can feel different animal furs, and an Observation Bee Hive. (The bees enter from outside, but you can watch the inner workings of the hive just behind the glass.) When you're out on the trails, you'll come across beaver dams, but in the Interpretive Building, there's a beaver dam that kids can crawl into (something not recommended in the wild). The exhibit gives kids a beaver's-eye view of life on a pond, complete with a heron catching fish.

After you've exhausted the exhibits, grab a trail map and head down the hill behind the building to the lakes. It almost doesn't matter what trail you take, as they're all interesting. Between Tree Top Pond and Little Pond is a tall A-frame bridge that's worth visiting. I've stood here and seen beaver and deer. Farther along that particular path, you come to a tower overlooking the aptly named Big Pond, and the return route is a long boardwalk through a cedar swamp. Before you leave, be sure to return to the main building and visit the Rookery—the center's gift shop and bookstore. It's a great way to support the organization, and they have a good selection of books on the natural history of Michigan.

It's a fact! The passenger pigeon went extinct because of a combination of factors—hunting, rapid loss of habitat, and the species' social nature. Passenger pigeons lived and traveled in large flocks, making them easy prey for hunters. Flocks also required swaths of uninterrupted woodlands, which quickly disappeared as the country was cleared for settlement.

18

Pine River Nature Center

TRAILS OPEN YEAR-ROUND, DAWN TO DUSK;
BUILDING OPEN WEEKDAYS, 8:30–4:30; FREE
2585 Castor Road, Goodells, MI 48027; (810) 364-5477;
www.sccresa.org/countyeducation/pine-river-nature-center

See for yourself! The nature center has a tree house that makes use of the dramatic terrain, and it's also accessible for everyone!

The rundown:

The Pine River Nature Center is owned and operated by the St. Clair County Regional Education Service Agency, and they host a lot of school groups and offer programs for students and scouts, as well as for the general public. The nature center sits on property just north of I-69, just outside of Goodells. The nature center is adjacent to the Goodells County Park, which straddles County Park Drive to the north.

The nature center building was constructed of logs and has a high vaulted ceiling and floor-to-ceiling windows that look out over the property. Inside there are wildlife exhibits and many birds on display, including specimens of a bald eagle and a turkey. Several aquariums house amphibians and reptiles, and there's even an indoor beehive.

The tree house is outside, of course. A wide wooden boardwalk leads out to the roomy building that is situated in the trees. Completely accessible, the tree house is a popular attraction for everyone. The property itself consists of 90 acres of hardwood forest, with a small grove of pines and some prairie. The Pine River runs through the preserve and contributes to the property's wetlands, which include oxbows and vernal ponds. More than 3 miles of trails wind through the park and all are clearly marked. Nature center staff recommends visitors wear long pants, no matter the season, to stay protected from insects and poison ivy. Because of the river, the property is very wet throughout the spring, so wear the right shoes if you plan to hike.

The nature center also maintains a reproduction American Indian village. This exhibit is intended to give visitors a feel for this part of the country before European settlement. There's a bark-covered wigwam, drying racks for animal skins and food, and a three sisters garden. A birch bark canoe is an apt addition. This close to the Pine River, canoes would have been necessary for transportation.

It's a fact! The Ojibwa (or, in their language, the *Anishinaabeg*) are part of the Council of Three Fires, an old alliance of the Ojibwa, the Ottawa, and the Potawatomi tribes. Descended from a single group that migrated west from the St. Lawrence River to the Upper Great Lakes, they often met at Michilimackinac to maintain regional peace.

19

DeVries Nature Conservancy

NATURE CENTER OPEN WEEKDAYS, 9–4;
TRAILS AND PLAYSCAPE OPEN DAILY DAWN TO DUSK; FREE
2635 North M-52, Owosso, MI 48867; (989) 723-3365;
www.devriesnature.org

See for yourself! The conservancy has restored a prairie on land once dedicated to agriculture. Throughout the summer you will find black-eyed Susans, purple coneflowers, and asters.

The rundown:

Located just minutes north of Owosso, the DeVries Nature Conservancy protects 136 acres along the Shiawassee River. The property was once the farm of Joseph DeVries, the local veterinarian, and his wife, Francis. The gift of land was supplemented with a healthy endowment to support its mission to "inspire curiosity and foster learning about Michigan's natural history and rural past."

The preserve features maple-beech forest, restored prairie, and floodplain, and it boasts 4 miles of trails. The lion's share of the property, however, is given over to cropland, and you may see the conservancy's Mobile Farmers Market around town. It delivers fresh seasonal produce to the wider community.

There are a number of ways to take advantage of the resources at DeVries. Children love the Kids Nature Playscape, which has a tree for climbing in addition to a climbing wall. There's also a slackline and a zip line for the younger kids. Another approach would be to come for a nature walk. There are trails that run down by the Shiawassee, and others follow the line between farmland and forest. Or you could visit the pollinator garden and watch the bees and butterflies go about their business. And if the gardening bug takes you, the conservancy rents out garden plots.

The Nature Center building is open on weekdays. Inside they have box turtles, a few snakes, an aquarium featuring river fish, and a hissing cockroach. When the nature center is staffed, ask if any of these critters want to come out and play. Outside they have rabbits and chickens.

The DeVries had a deep love for horse-drawn sleigh rides. Mr. DeVries, in fact, collected historic carriages and sleighs. That collection is preserved at the DeVries Conservancy in the Sleigh and Carriage Museum. There are 25 restored vehicles in all—from buggies and surreys to sleighs and cutters. It is considered one of the best museums of its kind in the Midwest. Visitors should note that the collection is only viewable by appointment.

It's a fact! The nearby town of Owosso was named for Chief Wasso, an Ojibwa leader who signed treaties in the early 1800s—the Treaty of Saginaw and the Treaty of Detroit—that ceded millions of acres to the US government.

20

Harris Nature Center

NATURE BUILDING OPEN IN SUMMER TUE.–FRI., 9–4; SAT., 12–4;
TRAILS OPEN DAILY, DAWN UNTIL DUSK; FREE
3998 Van Atta Road, Okemos, MI 48864; (517) 349-3866;
www.meridian.mi.us/harrisnaturecenter

See for yourself! The nature center takes in a lot of animals—from box turtles to red-tailed hawks. Many are temporary guests, but others are more long-term. You will see them on display in the nature center and around the building.

The rundown:

Meridian Township, east of Lansing, has developed a series of parks along the Red Cedar River. They are—from east to west—Legg Park, the Harris Nature Center, and Eastgate Park. Combined, they total 204 acres and are often referred to jointly as Meridian Riverfront Park. Nearly 3 miles of the Red Cedar are included in these properties. Each has its own nature trails, and they all connect, offering hikers a decently long walk.

The Harris Nature Center is the center link in this chain of parks. It offers educational programs, guided walks, programs for families, and summer day camps. The building itself is small, but its collection of live animals on display is definitely worth a visit. There are box turtles and map turtles, milk snakes and tiger salamanders. It's also where you go to pick up maps or to rent a GPS unit for geocaching. Next to the building is a natural playscape for the kids. It features a turtle structure, a rope spider-web, and more.

Starting from the nature center, there are a couple miles of nature trails that head north along the Red Cedar River from the center. The shortest of the lot is the paved White Spruce Loop. You pick up the trail at the north end of the parking lot. It takes a lollipop-shaped route through the woods and returns you to the parking lot. The other nature trails cut closer to the Red Cedar River and by choosing the right route, visitors can hike about a mile north to Eastgate Park on Meridian Road. Another set of trails can be found west of Van Atta Road in Legg Park.

Much of this property is a floodplain. In the spring, or when there's been a lot of rain, sections of the trail disappear or become too wet for walking. What's bad for hiking, however, is great for paddling, and there's a canoe launch at the Harris Nature Center for visitors who bring a boat. The center encourages visitors to stay on the trails at all times. Geocachers will want to take note: If you are planting a geocache, a permit is required in advance.

It's a fact! Lansing was built near the swampy confluence of two rivers. Not the most advantageous spot for a state capitol, the location was chosen because champions for other cities found Lansing less objectionable than having the capitol given to a rival.

21

Fenner Nature Center

TRAILS OPEN 8–SUNSET; VISITOR CENTER TUES.-FRI., 10-4; SAT.-SUN., 12-4.; FREE;
SUGGESTED DONATION FOR THE VISITOR CENTER IS $2/ADULT AND $1/CHILDREN
2020 East Mount Hope Avenue, Lansing, MI 48910; (517) 483-4224
www.mynaturecenter.org

See for yourself! Fenner has one of the last remaining groves of American chestnut trees in North America. The stand only has a couple dozen trees, but this is a chance to see the tree that once covered the eastern United States from Maine to Georgia. North American chestnuts were almost eradicated by the spread of chestnut blight in the early years of the twentieth century.

The rundown:

The area around the confluence of the Red Cedar River and Sycamore Creek, southeast of downtown Lansing, is littered with green spaces. It's home to the Potter Park Zoo as well as a pair of public parks: Scotts Woods and Hawk Island. Crego Park is just to the northeast and that's where you'll find the 134-acre Fenner Nature Center.

The visitor center here was recently renovated, and the new exhibits were designed to engage the public. There's been special attention paid to accommodate visitors who might not be fluent in English or who have disabilities that make it impractical to take a nature walk on the park's trails. One of the displays even features live animals—the center's collection of Michigan reptiles and amphibians. Most of the exhibits are hands-on, and children are encouraged to engage to their hearts' content.

Beyond the visitor center, Fenner has 4 miles of trails. Two of the trails are paved and fully accessible for those with disabilities or families with kids in strollers. This property was once all farmland, so the trees, shrubs, and plants you see were planted later—including the grove of American chestnuts. The nature center also has three manmade ponds, wetlands, a native prairie, and woodlands. A glacial esker, a long ridge left behind by a glacier, also runs through the park.

There are several spots of interest throughout the park. The Sugar Maple Trail passes by the property's many sugar maples. There is also a butterfly garden, an herb garden, a bridge that spans Field Pond, observation decks on Woodland Pond, and nice picnic facilities.

It's a fact! It is believed that eskers formed when melted water flowed through tunnels underneath glaciers. Sediment built up in the tunnels, like it does in any stream or river, and when the glacier retreated, the sediment was left behind, creating long, serpentine ridges.

22

Woldumar Nature Center

OPEN YEAR-ROUND. OPEN ON SAT. IN THE WINTER;
WED.–SUN. IN THE SUMMER; FRI.–SUN. DURING THE SHOULDER SEASONS;
CHECK SITE FOR HOURS; SUGGESTED $2 DONATION FOR USE OF TRAILS
5739 Old Lansing Road, Lansing, MI 48917; (517) 322-0030;
www.woldumar.org

See for yourself! Come see the Moon Cabin, one of the oldest homes in Eaton County. It has been restored to the way it would have looked in the 1860s.

The rundown:

The nature center's life dates back to the 1960s when Gladys Marguerite Olds Anderson, the daughter of Oldsmobile founder Ransom Eli Olds, donated a portion of her dairy farm to the Woldumar Nature Association to create a place where kids could learn about conservation. As gifts of property go, this location on the Grand River, southwest of downtown Lansing, was very generous.

All told, Woldumar has 178 acres of wetlands, prairie, and woods as well as 5 miles of trails. The Woodland Trail, for example, is a 1.5-mile loop that wanders through beech-maple forest, a pine plantation, a mixed forest, and the park's walnut glen (a secluded valley). The 1.4-mile Prairie Trail, on the other hand, skirts the woods and ventures along with a view of Woldumar's tallgrass prairie. The Mixed Forest Trail grazes the Grand River and gives hikers a closer view of the nearby "lagoon"—so named on the maps. There is also a 3/4-mile accessible trail called the Meadows Trail.

Though the nature center's mission is to "educate people about the natural environment," it also dedicates a good deal of effort to cultural education. This is apparent in the center's various buildings. There is the original barn that came with the property, which is primarily rented out for events. A coal-fired forge, which originally served a blacksmith in Waucousta, Michigan, is now used by the Blacksmiths of Woldumar to demonstrate blacksmithing. One of the property's most interesting structures is the Moon Log Cabin. Built in the late 1860s, this home was still occupied well into the twentieth century. Next to the cabin is an herb garden, which has been planted to represent a family garden circa the 1870s.

Trail maps and brochures are all available at the visitor center near the parking lot. The visitor center also houses the WolduMarket Gift Shop, one of the best-managed and best-stocked nature center shops I've come across.

It's a fact! The Grand River is Michigan's longest river. With a short portage, paddlers once traveled up the Huron River from Lake Erie and connected with the Grand River; this took them all the way to Lake Michigan and saved a paddle up and around the tip of the mitt.

23

Kalamazoo Nature Center

VISITOR CENTER MON.–SAT., 9–5; SUN., 1–5; TRAILS, 9–7:30;
MEMBERS FREE, ADULTS $7, CHILDREN (4–17) $4
7000 North Westnedge Avenue, Kalamazoo, MI 49009; (269) 381-1574;
www.naturecenter.org

See for yourself! You can help with the chores at the DeLano Homestead Farms. A few times a week, visitors get to help the staff feed Neo the pig, Lacey the Horse, and the center's other barnyard animals.

The rundown:

Located on the Kalamazoo River, about 5 miles north of town, the Kalamazoo Nature Center has many different personalities. It's an interpretive building with exhibits that teach visitors about ecosystems around the world, a gracefully landscaped arboretum and sculpture garden, a nature preserve crisscrossed by miles of trails, a historic homestead, and a working farm with live animals. Perhaps most importantly, it is a playground where kids can exercise their legs, arms, and imaginations.

The Visitor Center was built in the woods on the park's east side. It is located next to Cooper's Glen. This beech-and-maple forest is bisected by the Trout Run Stream, which meanders down to the Kalamazoo River, has been attracting people for centuries. Indigenous groups once camped here, and when European settlers arrived, they too saw the value of the spot. A long bridge takes you out to the upper level of the Visitor Center. A fantastic exhibit hall circles around a central atrium. The exhibits are hands-on, with places to explore, videos to watch, and plenty of things to read. The two-story atrium in the middle houses the center's Sun-Rain Room, simulating the warm humid environment of the tropics for the many plants inside. There are balconies overlooking the upper level with a stairway that leads to the downstairs exhibits. From this level you can head out to some of the trails.

Across from the Visitor Center is the arboretum. This area is landscaped with creative use of stones, trellises, and sculptures. There is a hummingbird-butterfly garden inside the arboretum that is worth seeing. Next to the arboretum is the kids' play area known as Nature's Playground. The playground has a stream, a water tower, and a lot of unstructured play areas. Adults without children in tow can forgo the play area and head right out to the trails. There are more than 10 miles of trails that wander through a mix of forest, prairies, and wetlands. The final stop should be the DeLano Homestead and Farm. It's located west of Westnedge Avenue. There is a lot of educational programming around the farm, and to get the most out of a visit, it's worth checking the calendar to see the event schedule.

It's a fact! The Kalamazoo River Valley Trail connects the nature center with downtown Kalamazoo and to points as far east as the River Oaks County Park in Galesburg.

24

Love Creek Nature Center

OPEN YEAR-ROUND. SUMMER HOURS WED.–SAT., 10–5; SUN., 1–5; TRAILS
DAWN TO DUSK; COUNTY RESIDENTS $3/VEHICLE; NONRESIDENTS $5/VEHICLE
9292 Huckleberry Road, Berrien Center, MI 49102; (269) 471-2617;
www.berriencounty.org/Parks/LoveCreek

See for yourself! In the winter, the park's hiking and mountain biking trails undergo a transformation. They become groomed cross-country skiing and fat-tire biking trails. If you don't have gear, don't worry: The park rents out skis and bikes.

The rundown:

For a time, the town of Berrien Springs was the county seat for Berrien County. The seat moved to St. Joe's in 1894, and today the village is best known as the home of Andrews University. The Love Creek County Park is located just a few miles east of downtown and the St. Joseph River. The 200-acre property features a sprawling beech-maple forest and the winding Love Creek.

Not far in from the park entrance is the Love Creek Nature Center, where you'll find experienced naturalists leading a variety of educational programs. A number of wildlife exhibits are inside the nature center; they include animal pelts that kids can touch, a microscope with slides of bug parts you can examine up close, and displays that teach about weasels and owls. A wall of aquariums houses the center's collection of live, native reptiles and amphibians. And from the main exhibit room, you can watch birds attracted to the birdfeeders outside.

Judging from how popular the trails are here, the real attraction is the cross-country skiing. Groups drive a long way to tackle these trails. They are marked out for classic and skate skiing, and they are also assigned difficulty ratings. In the summer, the trails are perfectly fine for hiking and mountain biking, though countless people have commented on the deer fly situation. If you're familiar with deer flies, you know what I am talking about. During the season, you'll need to dress appropriately and wear bug spray.

All told, the park maintains 6 miles of trails. The terrain is varied—rolling hills blanketed with a thick beech-maple forest. The woods are home to many spring ephemerals. While the weather is still cool, it's a great time to learn about wildflowers.

It's a fact! Nearby Berrien Springs was originally named for John M. Berrien, a US senator from Georgia and one-time attorney general under Andrew Jackson. Later, mineral springs were discovered nearby and "Springs" was added to the name.

25

Fernwood Botanical Garden and Nature Preserve

MAY–OCT. TUE.–SAT., 10–6; SUN., NOON–6; CLOSES AT 5 FROM NOV.–APR.;
MEMBERS FREE, ADULTS $7, CHILDREN (5–17) $4
13988 Range Line Road, Niles, MI 49120; (269) 695-6491;
www.fernwoodbotanical.org

See for yourself! Come for Sculpture at Fernwood, a curated collection of art on exhibit throughout the gardens. Of particular note is the large twig sculpture titled "Take Five," woven from willow branches.

The rundown:

Many nature preserves have relatively few buildings and structures. Aside from a nature center building, trails with interpretive signage, and a garden or two, nature is presented without ornament. Fernwood, however, isn't just a nature preserve; it's also a botanical garden and an arboretum. Its wild spaces are as important as its beautifully landscaped gardens. Here you find forested trails crossing creeks and running alongside the St. Joseph River, but there are also manicured lawns, sculpted trees, a Japanese garden, a cottage garden, an herb garden, as well as carefully selected artwork.

The Visitor Center is the gateway to the property. It's where guests pay the entrance fee and pick up a site map. There's a really nice gift shop, and Fernwood also hosts regular plant sales for gardeners. The Clark Gallery features the work of different artists every few months. The visitor center also features a café that serves soups and sandwiches and has indoor and outdoor seating.

Visiting the gardens could be an activity for an entire afternoon. Kids will particularly enjoy the Railway Garden and the Nature Adventure Garden. The former features four model trains running on different levels of track. There are bridges and ponds and tunnels. All told, there are 510 feet of track. There's even a tunnel just for kids that leads to the Nature Adventure Garden. There, natural materials have been used to create a playscape for children, one that taps the need for unstructured play—paths, tunnels, hobbit houses, and stick structures abound. There are numerous other gardens to explore, plus the "Take Five" twig sculpture. Farther back in the woods, toward the St. Joseph River, you'll find the Ravine Garden, the Water Wheel, and the Corkscrew Bridge. And beyond that, the Ecology Trail leads down and around the Big Pond.

There is a Nature Center on the property, but the best experience is on the hiking trails. The nature preserve, arboretum, and tall-grass prairie are all found north of the gardens and require some walking. Hiking both the Wilderness Trail and the Arboretum Loop is a nice way to view the entire property.

It's a fact! Long used by American Indians, the French first traveled the St. Joseph river in 1654. Both Marquette and LaSalle paddled the river, as did countless fur traders.

26

ENTERING

WARREN WOODS NATIONAL

NATURAL LANDMARK

Caution

Warren Woods Natural Area

DAILY, 8–DUSK;
THE MICHIGAN RECREATION PASSPORT IS REQUIRED (SEE PAGE 7)
Elm Valley Road, Three Oaks, MI 49128; (269) 426-4013;
www.michigandnr.com/parksandtrails/details.aspx?id=505&type=SPRK

See for yourself! This park has 100-foot-tall beech trees; many are more than 450 years old!

The rundown:

Warren Woods State Park is home to the state's last virgin stand of beech-maple forest. A designated nature area and national natural landmark, the park features a single trail that begins at the parking area and ends at the trailhead on Warren Woods Road to the north.

The path cuts through a forest of nearly 200 acres (the park itself is 311 acres) and, along the way, it crosses a bridge over the Galien River. Some of the towering beeches here are more than 450 years old, which means they would have been saplings when William Shakespeare was a baby. The smooth-barked silver beeches rise 100 feet from the forest floor to create a canopy overhead. The shorter sugar maple trees that populate the forest understory gather up what little light trickles through the leaves above them.

The fact that Warren Woods still exists is remarkable and due to the foresight and generosity of a nineteenth-century businessman from Three Rivers. Mr. E. K. Warren purchased the property in 1878 with the intent to save the woods for posterity. He kept possession of the land, even when he faced times of financial difficulty, but then he hit upon an idea—using feathers instead of whalebone in corsets—and this made him very wealthy. He used his newfound wealth to add to his legacy of conservation by buying up "worth-less" dune land on Lake Michigan—property that is now Warren Dunes State Park.

The trail here is easy to follow and easy to walk. There is some elevation gain, but it's minimal, and there are stairs for areas with moderate climbs. It's part of the park's mission to remain undeveloped; so aside from the path, there are very few amenities—pit toilets and a picnic table or two are about it. Nonetheless, that adds to the allure, as this is largely a wild place. The forest here takes on different colors and a different atmosphere with the changing of the seasons, so while there might not be a lot of bells and whistles, the park is worth more than one visit.

It's a fact! Prior to the invention of "featherbone," corsets—once a must-have accessory for women—were made with whalebone, which became increasingly rare as whale populations were basically wiped out by whaling. Warren's "featherbone" was made instead from turkey "pointer" feathers that he acquired from feather duster factories in Chicago, which usually discarded them.

27

Sarett Nature Center

CENTER BUILDING OPEN SUN., 1–5; TUE.–FRI., 9–5; SAT., 1–5;
TRAILS DAILY DAWN TO DUSK; KIDS 12 AND UNDER FREE, NONMEMBER ADULTS $3
2300 North Benton Center Road, Benton Harbor, MI 49022; (269) 927-4832;
www.sarett.com

See for yourself! One of the best parts of a nature walk at Sarett is a very short walk from the parking area. As you walk the path out to the end of the Tree Top Tower, you'll find yourself on a wooden walkway; beneath you, the ground drops away and you find yourself 55 feet above the landscape. For a time, you literally walk through the canopy and get a bird's-eye view of the valley below, a pretty incredible sight.

The rundown:

When I was younger, the kids in my neighborhood swam in the Paw Paw River, sometimes floating down long stretches on hot summer days. While the Sarett Nature Center is miles from my childhood digs, I was excited to find the old river flowing nearby the center, which is located just a few miles northeast of Benton Harbor.

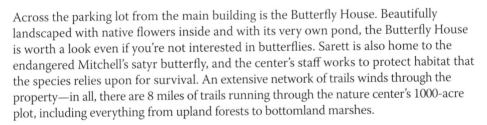

The Sarett Nature Center's main building has room for classes and meetings as well as exhibits about wildlife. Don't miss the center's Wood Shop and its weekend woodworking courses; part of the fun of woodworking is partnering with nature to make something useful. The center also has a table where kids can pick up shells from various creatures. The center's aquariums hold turtles, and farther down the hall you will find a nook housing various nonvenomous snakes.

Across the parking lot from the main building is the Butterfly House. Beautifully landscaped with native flowers inside and with its very own pond, the Butterfly House is worth a look even if you're not interested in butterflies. Sarett is also home to the endangered Mitchell's satyr butterfly, and the center's staff works to protect habitat that the species relies upon for survival. An extensive network of trails winds through the property—in all, there are 8 miles of trails running through the nature center's 1000-acre plot, including everything from upland forests to bottomland marshes.

In addition to the Tree Top Tower, there are other towers at Sarett. Return visits might be necessary to really scout out the entire preserve. And after that? Well, the Sarett Nature Center owns two other properties along the Paw Paw River—Black's Woods and the Brown Sanctuary—both of which are open to the public. Just check the website for directions.

It's a fact! The Paw Paw River was named by American Indians long before settlers arrived here. It was named for the many paw paw trees that grew along its banks. The trees produce—wouldn't you guess it?—paw paw fruit, which is something of a regional specialty.

28

Outdoor Discovery Center/Macatawa Greenway

SUN., 12–4, MON.–FRI., 9–5; SAT., 10–4; TRAILS DAILY DAWN TO DUSK; FREE
4214 56th Street, Holland, MI 49423; (616) 393-9453;
www.outdoordiscovery.org

See for yourself! The Imagination Forest Children's Play Area doesn't feature your everyday playground equipment. Instead, the site has a natural playscape that features logs, tunnels, and creative plantings, an approach that increases cooperative play among children.

The rundown:

Hunters are some of the most passionate conservation advocates around. (Just think of Teddy Roosevelt.) As a case in point, this Outdoor Discovery Center was founded by Wildlife Unlimited, one such conservation-minded group. As such, the center focuses a lot on hunting and fishing. The main building—the Discovery Pavilion—houses two rooms of taxidermy mounts—including bison, mountain lions, elk, fish, and more. There is also a display on the history of hunting with examples of different rifles used throughout the years. Of course, the taxidermy specimens are not the only wildlife to be found at the center. Behind the pavilion is a fenced-in enclosure that houses the center's herd of Rocky Mountain elk. Right next to the pavilion is the Imagination Forest Children's Play Area. There are logs to climb and a tunnel to explore. There is even a child-size log cabin with a kitchen and a loft. If you have a family in tow, this playscape will hold kids' attention for quite a while.

The Discovery Center property includes several different ecosystems, from marshland and transitional hardwood forest to remnant dunes and restored prairies. The preserve also has a network of paths that lead to outdoor classrooms and the fishing pond. The Sensory Trail Loop is the closest one to the main facilities. Just beyond the loop you come to the center's Neshnabe Summer Village, which is inspired by the Anishinaabe people who originally inhabited the area. It features a traditional cookhouse, a bent-pole wigwam, and a three sisters garden consisting of corn, pole beans, and squash. The Outdoor Discovery Center recently merged with the Macatawa Greenway, a network of permanently protected land along the river, making the site an even better place to visit.

Farther into the park you will come to the Birds of Prey Education Facility, adjacent to the Little Hawks Discovery Preschool. (Visitors with disabilities can park in the preschool lot, skipping the walk.) All of the 12 birds in the facility have a permanent injury and cannot be returned to the wild. Instead eagles, owls and other birds that live here help educate visitors about birds of prey.

It's a fact! Once found throughout Michigan, elk were extirpated from much of their former range. They were later re-introduced from the Rocky Mountains; the Outdoor Discovery Center is home to a Rocky Mountain elk population.

29

Degraaf Nature Center

BUILDING OPEN TUE.–FRI., 9–5; SAT., 10–5;
TRAILS OPEN DAILY DAWN TO DUSK; FREE
600 Graafschap Road, Holland, MI 49423; (616) 355-1057;
www.degraaf.org

See for yourself! In December, the Degraaf Nature Center hosts a pioneer Christmas in the old log cabin. This is a time of crafts and snacks, warm fires, and a little education about life in the nineteenth century.

The rundown:

Tucked into a quiet Holland neighborhood, across from a church, and once hidden behind a house, this isn't the first place you would look for preserved green space. And even sitting in the parking lot, it's hard to imagine that there's an 18-acre preserve with woods, marshes, and ponds on site.

This isn't where people are going to come to train for a half marathon—18 acres is a decent size, but it's not a massive amount of space. Instead, people come here to observe and experience nature. The well-groomed loop trail that winds through the property's best features is laid with boardwalks and other hard-packed surfaces, which is good news for families with strollers and guests with wheelchairs. The boardwalks provide a dry path over the wetlands, and there are places where visitors can reach down and feel the stream as it passes through.

Back at the nature center building, there are some excellent wildlife exhibits. There are detailed dioramas populated with stuffed foxes and ducks. Above you, a turkey is frozen in flight. There are live critters as well—snakes and turtles and small animals—and the site plays host to other animals that are brought in from time to time for educational purposes.

There's also a historic aspect to the nature center. It features a log cabin that is home to all sorts of classes and demonstrations, much of it focusing on nineteenth-century Holland.

It's a fact! Macatawa Lake is fed by the Macatawa River. Macatawa is the Ottawa and Potawatomi word for black. The name comes from the water, which has been stained dark by tannins from decayed vegetation.

30

Nature Education Center at Hemlock Crossing Park

SUN., 12–5; TUE.–SAT., 9–5; PARK DAILY, 7–10 MAR.–OCT. AND 7–8 OCT.–FEB.;
FREE; 8115 West Olive Road, West Olive, MI 49460; (616) 786-4847;
www.miottawa.org/parks/hemlockcrossing.htm

See for yourself! Hemlock Crossing has a kayak launch, and you can tour the property with a nice paddle down the Pigeon River. If you want to rent a boat, contact the park, as it can put you in touch with area outfitters.

The rundown:

Hemlock Crossing Park is stretched along the Pigeon River east of Port Sheldon. The main entrance is just off US 31, halfway between Grand Haven and Holland. (There's also trailhead parking at the western end of the park.) For families like ours who are always trying to find ways to add value to our road trips, Hemlock Crossing is a very convenient stop. You could come for a quick half hour of looking around the Nature Education Center or stay for the afternoon and explore the trails.

If the Nature Education Center at the park is not the newest nature center in this book, it's darn close. Construction was completed in 2010. The center has a host of nature exhibits and a hands-on focus for kids. The programming has a similar approach and helps families get a personal look at the park's wild inhabitants, which includes everything from turkeys to foxes. After taking a gander inside, kids can head outdoors and see the animals' habitat first-hand.

Hemlock Crossing Park consists of 239 acres along the Pigeon River, including grasslands, forests, and wetlands. Nearly 7 miles of trails run through the park. One of the more interesting trail sections is very close to the nature center. Heading north from the center, you quickly come to a boardwalk and bridge over the river. It's a very peaceful spot, and it's no wonder that the first of the park's 7 scenic viewing areas is right here.

Paddlers will want to explore the Pigeon River from the water. The park has a kayak launch (near the main entrance) for easy access to the river, and it's only a short 2.5-hour paddle from the park to Port Sheldon Park on Lake Michigan. Outfitters in Grand Haven and Holland deliver to Hemlock Crossing, so you don't even need to own a kayak to partake.

It's a fact! The Pigeon River that flows through Hemlock Crossing Park gets its name from the once-ubiquitous passenger pigeon, which called Michigan home.

31

Gillette Sand Dune Visitor Center at Hoffmaster State Park

SUN., 12–5; MON.–SAT., 10–5; FREE
6585 Lake Harbor Road, Muskegon, MI 49441; (231) 798-3573;
www.gillettenature.org

See for yourself! You might think that dunes are only found in deserts or in far-flung places like the Sahara, but you can see them right here in Michigan at Hoffmaster State Park. It's also home to 3 miles of sandy beach!

The rundown:

Located about halfway between Muskegon and Grand Haven, Hoffmaster State Park is perched on the dunes overlooking Lake Michigan. The north section of the park houses a campground with modern and semi-modern sites, as well as a day-use area with easy access to the beach. The Gillette Sand Dune Visitor Center is found in the southern half of Hoffmaster, adjacent to the park's designated natural area. The center has a wing dedicated to the natural and human history of the surrounding dunes.

The exhibits show how dunes are formed and how they change over the years. Different dune residents, such as the antlion, get some time in the spotlight. This predator creates funnel-like traps in the sand, waiting just below the surface to pounce on any poor insect that wanders in. A scaled-up model of the antlion is accompanied by a short video. Other exhibits look at the pioneers of dune conservation; the bottom level of the visitor center has a small room dedicated to invasive species, such as the sea lamprey and the zebra mussel.

The visitor center has different things going all the time, and you won't necessarily find them on the calendar. On my last visit, for example, a taxidermist was sewing up a turtle and explaining the process while guests looked on. From the visitor center parking lot you can also link up with a number of trails and paths. Some lead out toward the water, up over the dunes and to a high dune lookout, and then through the wooded backdunes. A visit to the park is incomplete without a hike up the Dune Climb Stairway. Though a little laborious, the panoramic view of the dunes at the top is worth the effort. There are also quite a few trails for more extended hikes.

Don't forget that Hoffmaster State Park has 3 miles of beach. You can drive back to the day-use area and park with the other beachgoers, or hike the Homestead Trail a half mile out from the visitor center. Don't forget to bring your suit!

It's a fact! Walking in from the beach over the dunes, you'll encounter several ecological zones; walking from a young, unformed beach to a mature forest is almost like walking through time.

77

32

Blandford Nature Center

VISITOR CENTER OPEN MON.–FRI., 9–5 AND SAT., 12–5;
TRAILS OPEN DAWN TO DUSK; NONMEMBERS $3; MEMBERS FREE
1715 Hillburn Avenue NW, Grand Rapids, MI 49504; (616) 735-6240;
www.blandfordnaturecenter.org

See for yourself! Blandford's heritage buildings will give you a taste of nineteenth-century life. See a blacksmith hammering out some horseshoes or tour the 1853 schoolhouse.

The rundown:

The Blandford Nature Center began as a 17-acre donation to the Grand Rapids Public Museum, and it's now an independent nonprofit organization of 143 acres. The center now encompasses creeks and wetlands as well as prairie, meadow, and forest. There are even historic buildings and a working farm. Wildflowers abound in the spring, and visitors have spotted a variety of birds, including snowy owls, egrets, pileated woodpeckers, and the iconic bald eagle. There are deer everywhere, as well as turtles and muskrat, and a host of other furry residents.

The center maintains more than 4 miles of trails. They're all divvied up into shorter loops, each less than a mile, so you can take a short walk or tack some loops together for a longer hike. The Brandywine Creek winds through the east portion of the property and meanders behind the current visitor center. Because of the wetlands, many of the trails feature boardwalks at times.

There's no substitute for getting out there on the trails for learning about nature, especially if you are participating in a guided walk, but the center also has some teaching facilities, like the newly constructed Visitor and Interpretive Center. There are also exhibits as well as a decent gift shop (a great way to support the center financially). This is also where you will find the Wildlife Education Center, which houses a number of animals that were injured and brought to Blandford for rehabilitation. Some were injured and couldn't survive in the wild, so they now reside at the center and participate in the center's wildlife education programs.

At Blandford, 2.5 acres of the site are dedicated to agriculture. (They have a barn and everything!) Blandford has its own CSA (community supported agriculture project) and sells produce in Grand Rapids at the Fulton Street Market. Blandford also has a robust calendar of programs and events for young and old. You will also want to take note of the nature center's "signature events." For example, in early spring you can attend the Sugarbush Festival, where visitors learn all about maple trees, harvesting sap, and boiling syrup.

It's a fact! About 40 gallons of sugar maple sap is needed to make 1 gallon of syrup. Other maples have less sugar, so even more sap is needed. If you want to get your hands on some, head to the gift shop; syrup made on site is available for sale.

33

Howard Christensen Nature Center

INTERPRETIVE CENTER SUMMER MON.–FRI., 9–4; WEEKENDS, 12–4
(CHECK SITE FOR WINTER HOURS); TRAILS DAWN TO DUSK; $3
16190 Red Pine Drive NW, Kent City, MI 49330; (616) 675-3158;
www.howardchristensen.org

See for yourself! A handful of wooden tower-like platforms give visitors a bird's-eye view of the property, making for great photo opportunities.

The rundown:

The Howard Christensen Nature Center (HCNC) is in a period of transition. The property is owned by the Kent Intermediate School District. A few years ago, however, the ISD lost funding for the nature center, and the property was shuttered. Fortunately for the thousands of schoolchildren (and many others) who have learned about Michigan flora and fauna at the HCNC, some volunteers set up a nonprofit to manage the site. Today, the nature center is still owned by the school district but operated by Lily's Frog Pad.

Surrounded by the Rogue River State Game Area, the HCNC consists of 135 acres tucked into the wilds of northwestern Kent County, exactly 20 miles north of downtown Grand Rapids. The facilities include a Welcome Center with restrooms, outdoor benches, and a newly remodeled Interpretive Center. The path to the Interpretive Center takes you down to a pond and across a floating bridge. Along the way you will pass an ornate tumbling stream and a boulder with a plaque dedicated to Howard Christensen, who died at 17; his family dedicated this property in his memory.

The HCNC is mighty proud of the work done on the Interpretive Center. A new Critter Room is a favorite with kids, and the Bird Room has mounted specimens of many Michigan birds. Quite a few of the birds in the collection are now extinct, which both serves as a way to learn about what we've lost and a reminder that we need to take ecology seriously. The center also maintains quite a few trails. There's a map on the wall of the Welcome Center near the parking area, and the trails are clearly marked. For a closer look at the site's wetlands, combine a couple of the hikes into a loop. For example, a nice short hike along the Chrishaven Boardwalk and the Nature's Habitat Trail takes you out to the Swamp Tower and Swamp Shelter. From there, the Swamp Ridge Trail brings you back.

Throughout the year, the HCNC runs dozens of programs for children, from field trips to special events. The organization also hosts a handful of classes geared toward adults; these classes provide an introduction to a wide variety of pursuits—from raising chickens and organic gardening to maintaining eco-friendly lawns and making beer and wine.

It's a fact! An early owner of the property, Carl Dunson, believed he had filled the site with at least one example of every native Michigan plant species. He also planted exotic species from around the world, which he found on his many travels.

34

Chippewa Nature Center

VISITOR CENTER MON.–SAT., 8–5; SUN., 12–5; TRAILS DAWN TO DUSK; FREE
400 South Badour Road, Midland, MI 48640; (989) 631-0830;
www.chippewanaturecenter.org

See for yourself! American Indians camped at the confluence of the Pine and Chippewa Rivers for hundreds of years. Visit the nature center's wigwam to get a sense of what life was like for the indigenous people who lived here.

The rundown:

The Chippewa Nature Center is one of the finest nature centers in the state and certainly the best in mid-Michigan. It encompasses 1,348 acres of forest and wetlands on the confluence of the Pine and Chippewa Rivers. The center's many oxbow lakes and ponds are evidence of the many paths these rivers once took. The nature center is not only a place to learn about natural history; it is also a place where visitors learn about human history—from the American Indians who lived here to the area's first European settlers.

For an introduction to the natural history of the area, start at the Visitor Center. There are some fine exhibits here that offer basic information about the woods, wetlands, and rivers in the park. Much of the space is geared toward kids with a lot of hands-on, interactive displays. Discovery stations give visitors a chance to hear bird calls or touch animal pelts or a turtle shell. Parents enjoy visiting at their own pace while their children are engaged in the "Kids Conifer Corner" with its puppets and puzzles.

Returning outdoors, the nature center maintains 15 miles of trails that wind through beech-maple forests and groves of oak, pine, and aspen. There are upland fields, rivers, and wetlands. Some of the loops have their own trailheads. For a really nice walk, follow the River Trail along the Chippewa River and return via the Homestead Trail. The whole loop comes to about 4 miles and it passes the Homestead Farm, which houses pigs, cows, and chickens. In addition to the log cabin and barn, there is also a one-room log schoolhouse and a sugarhouse from the 1870s. On weekends in March, visitors can stop by the sugarhouse to see how maple syrup is made. The other historical structure at the center is the wigwam. Throughout the year, a number of classes are held at the wigwam, usually focusing on traditional skills.

The Chippewa Nature Center also hosts many other events, activities, classes, and seminars. It's worth spending some time browsing their website if you want to get something extra out of your visit.

It's a fact! The Oxbow you see on the map of the Chippewa Nature Center was once part of the Chippewa River. In 1912, a flood carved a new path for the river and left this small lake behind.

35

Huron County Nature Center
& Wilderness Arboretum

TRAILS OPEN YEAR-ROUND DAWN-DUSK; VISITOR CENTER
OPEN MEMORIAL DAY THROUGH LABOR DAY, SAT., 10–4; SUN., 12–4; FREE
Loosemore Road, Port Austin, MI 48467; (989) 551-8400;
www.huronnaturecenter.org

See for yourself! If you're a birder, head here! An official stop on the Saginaw Bay Birding Trail (www.sblc-mi.org/bird.html), the nature center is home to a variety of woodland birds, as well as songbirds, raptors, and waterfowl.

The rundown:

The northern tip of Michigan's "thumb" is probably best known for its beaches and festivals. The Huron County Nature Center focuses on the abundant natural beauty found inland. When European settlers first came to this part of the state, they were met by a forest that spread beyond the horizon. Lumberman came, the forests fell, and fires followed, and eventually the region took on the agricultural character you see now. The nature center and accompanying arboretum seek to capture the area's natural history by preserving this forest as a place of retreat, education, and study.

While the trees here are huge, according to the folks at the nature center, none of the trees were planted before 1881. That makes sense. In 1881, the Great Thumb Fire swept through here and razed everything in its path. The property was probably also hit 10 years earlier by the Great Michigan Fire, and it was perhaps even logged before that. All of the fires that struck this area can be attributed to the logging industry. When clearing a forest, logging companies had no need for the thin top portions of trees they felled, so they left the branches, rich with combustible pine sap, behind. This created millions of acres of tinder.

The Huron County Nature Center is located between Port Austin and Caseville on Loosemore Road (just east of Oak Beach Road). The site preserves 280 acres, including a 120-acre wilderness arboretum. Well-marked trails climb upland wooded ridges, pass over low wet swales and wetland areas, and offer scenic overlooks for taking it all in. There's a separate loop to the north of the entrance that is accessible for visitors with disabilities.

The Nature Center hosts programs each Saturday in the summer; programs start at 10:30 and they vary each week. One morning there might be a bug hunt or a mammal expert flanked by a table of animal skulls. You can check out the schedule on the website.

It's a fact! October 8, 1871, was the day of the Peshtigo Fire in Wisconsin, the Chicago Fire, and the Great Michigan Fire that burned in Holland and Manistee as well as in Port Huron. Ten years later, the Great Thumb Fire struck this part of Michigan again, burning more than a million acres in a single day.

Northern Lower Peninsula

36

THE EXPLOITERS

HORNS or ANTLERS?

Johnson Hunting and Fishing Center at William Mitchell State Park

MEMORIAL DAY TO DECEMBER 1, OPEN DAILY, 10–6;
DECEMBER 1 TO MEMORIAL DAY, OPEN FRI., 12–5; SAT.–SUN., 11–5;
NATURE AREA OPEN YEAR-ROUND DURING DAYLIGHT HOURS;
MICHIGAN RECREATION PASSPORT REQUIRED (PAGE 7)
6087 East M-115, Cadillac, MI 49601; (231) 779-1321;
www.michigan.gov/huntfishcenter

See for yourself! Exhibits here detail the history of hunting—looking back to the earliest human hunters—with a focus on the contributions the hunting and fishing communities have made to conservation efforts.

The rundown:

Mitchell State Park encompasses 334 acres and is tucked neatly between Lake Mitchell and Lake Cadillac and straddling the Cadillac Canal. The park campground is south of the canal. To the north is the Carl T. Johnson Hunting and Fishing Center and the Cadillac Heritage Nature Study Area.

The Carl T. Johnson Hunting and Fishing Center provides a great introduction to Michigan's fish and wildlife. Located at the corner of M-115 and North Boulevard, the center overlooks the canal. The center's unique focus on hunting and fishing sets it apart from most nature centers. The exhibit space is stocked with animals, many taken from the area. The large aquarium is stocked with fish caught by kids in the nearby canal and features largemouth bass, bluegill, and yellow perch, among others.

Other exhibits include a large interactive fishing simulator, a marsh diorama, kiosks with audio clips about state wildlife and the various habitats that support it, and dioramas that illustrate the history of hunting and fishing in Michigan. There's a particular emphasis on the role sportsmen and women played in protecting wildlife habitat. In addition to interpretive facilities, the center offers a schedule of classes as part of the Outdoor Skills Academy. Participants can learn how to cast a fly, how to hunt, and more.

To explore outdoors, the 2.5-mile Mitchell-Heritage Nature Trail can be picked up from the visitor center or the east end of the parking lot. A half-mile trek takes you back to the Cadillac Heritage Nature Study Area. Black Creek flows between the two lakes on either side of the park; it also feeds the 70-acre Heritage Marsh. The paths here follow a rather regular route around the marsh, though one path passes through the middle of the wetlands, and another leads out to a viewing platform.

It's a fact! All 1,150 acres of Lake Cadillac lie inside the city limits. The lake is famous for its prolific bass fishing, and it's the site of many bass tournaments.

37

Green Point Dunes Nature Preserve

OPEN YEAR-ROUND, DAWN TO DUSK; FREE
Green Point Road, Frankfort, MI 49635; (231) 929-7911;
www.gtrlc.org/recreation-events/preserve/green-point-dunes-nature-preserve

See for yourself! If the day is clear and the water not too choppy, you can hike out to the bluff and look down to see the hull of the *City of Boston*, which ran aground and sank in Lake Michigan in 1873.

The rundown:

The Green Point Dunes Nature Preserve protects 242 rolling acres along Lake Michigan. There are backdunes, forested with white birch or beech and maple, and open meadows that come alive with wildflowers in the spring. There are also open foredunes that overlook 2,100 feet of sandy Lake Michigan beach. Half of the preserve has been designated a "critical dune" by the state, which means it's a fragile but important area.

From the parking area on Green Point Road, a 3-mile lollipop of a trail leads out through the woods, along the top of a steep bluff, and then to the beach. Along the way you pass two scenic viewing platforms. From this height you can look south and see Lower Herring Lake and the Arcadia Dunes. To the west, the outline of the *City of Boston* is visible in Lake Michigan.

The *City of Boston* ran aground about 3 miles south of Frankfort on November 20, 1873, in one of the lake's late autumn snowstorms. Thankfully, the crew was saved, but the ship and its cargo—corn and flour—were lost. The *Buffalo Commercial Advertiser* later reported, "There have been countless thousands of wild ducks on the lake during the winter feeding on her cargo of corn." Interestingly, the *City of Boston* was wrecked twice. The first time, in 1868, she collided with another boat and sank in 125 feet of water. When they raised the ship in 1870, it was the deepest salvage operation ever on the Great Lakes.

Before the trail turns eastward back into the woods, you will see stairs that will take you down to the water below. Few beaches on Lake Michigan in the summer are as quiet as this remote preserve; the hike probably puts some people off. Those who do make the trek come to swim or laze on the beach, hike or run the trails, or simply take in nature.

The property is managed by the Grand Traverse Regional Land Conservancy, which has set this tract aside as a natural space, saving it from development forever.

It's a fact! Certain species of plants have adapted to survive the dune environment. They resist abrasion from the wind-blown sand and continue to grow even when buried.

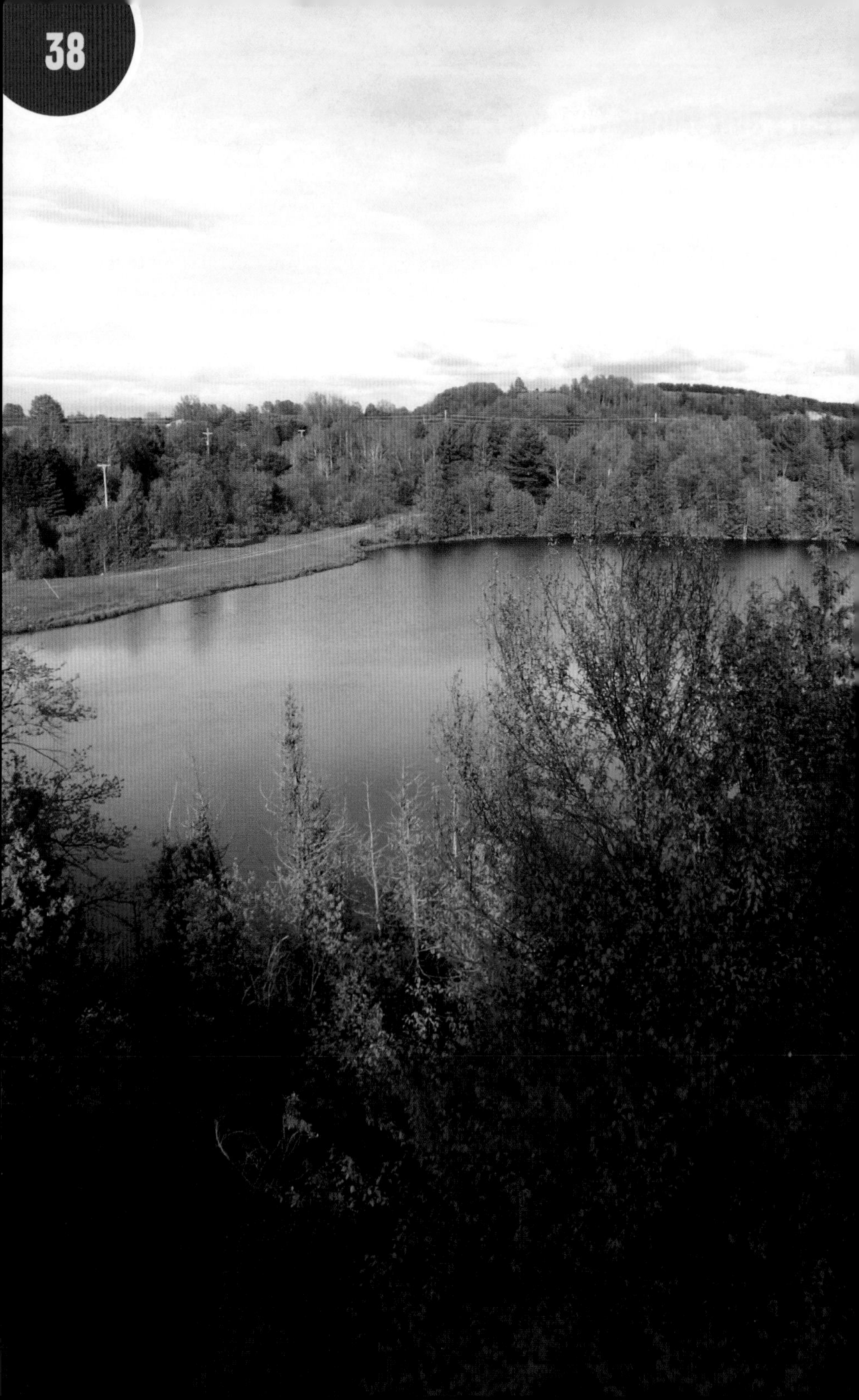

38

Boardman River Nature Center

NATURE CENTER TUE.–FRI., 10–4; SATURDAYS, JUNE THROUGH SEPT.; FREE
1450 Cass Road, Traverse City, MI 49685; (231) 941-4263;
natureiscalling.org/explore/nature-center/

See for yourself! The center's Fossil Exhibit takes you back 360 million years, introducing you to what lived here when this part of the world was underwater.

The rundown:

Overlooking Grand Traverse Bay, Traverse City sits on one of Michigan's most beautiful spots. Thousands come every summer for the area's festivals, food, and farm-fresh produce. The Boardman River runs right through the heart of town. Its banks have been heavily transformed within the city, and it makes some interesting turns as it cuts under and behind Front Street and tucks in next to parking lots before emptying into the bay. Farther upstream, however, the river takes on a wilder character.

The Grand Traverse Natural Education Reserve consists of 505 acres along the Boardman River, running from South Airport Road (just south of town) to Beitner Road. The reserve is primarily on the west side of the river, though south of Boardman Pond; it also includes the east bank. Throughout the reserve you will find upland forest, wetlands, and meadows. These provide habitat for foxes, deer, mink and river otters. Beaver live here as well, and there is an active beaver pond. There are also 7 miles of trails for hiking and exploring.

The gateway to all this natural wonder is the Boardman River Nature Center on Cass Road. The nature center has a fine collection of native Michigan flora and fauna. The Fossil Exhibit is one of the center's newer additions and takes you back 360 million years. You can learn why Petoskey stones have their unique pattern and find out what lived here when this whole area was underwater.

The nature center garden features native plants, and the butterfly garden is a certified monarch butterfly way station. To really appreciate the reserve, plan on taking one of their guided tours of the trails along the Boardman River.

Because the reserve is spread out along the river, not all the trails are easily accessible from one trailhead. You will find parking areas and trailheads where the property crosses roads; they have a map of these trails available online or at the nature center.

It's a fact! Like many rivers in the area, the Boardman River has many dams. One of the effects of damming a river is that the resulting ponds and lakes increase the temperature of the water. This creates problems for fish that need cold water to survive. Dams on the Boardman River are being removed, thus restoring an important natural ecosystem.

39

Grass River Natural Area

DAILY, 6–8; FREE
6500 Alden Highway, Bellaire, MI 49615; (231) 533-8576;
www.grassriver.org

See for yourself! Enjoy getting lost amid the preserve's maze of boardwalks. They meander through a dense cedar swamp, where shallow, incredibly clear, sandy-bottomed creeks flow just beneath your feet. Here, you'll find yourself literally surrounded by forest.

The rundown:

At Grass River Natural Area, the trails are what you've come to see. Visitors have a lot of variety to choose from: You can walk through a cedar swamp, a sedge meadow, or an upland forest. The boardwalks through the cedar swamp are especially interesting. Shallow, sandy-bottomed streams flow through this part of the property. The undergrowth is so thick that when you come to different sections of flowing water, it's hard to tell if you're upstream or downstream from the last section you stumbled upon. Or maybe it's a different stream altogether. There's something downright fairy-tale like about these trails.

One trail leads out to a dock overlooking Grass River, and there are longer loops to the south. A natural inventory of the site counted hundreds of different plant species, as well as dozens of different birds, mammals, reptiles, amphibians, and fish. In terms of mammals, Grass River is even more impressive. They have the usual opossums, woodchucks, and white-tailed deer, but some of the animals spotted here are almost exotic by downstate standards: black bear, snowshoe hare, bobcat, beaver, and river otter, not to mention weasel and mink.

All tallied, the Grass River Natural Area is close to 1,500 acres, and it includes the entirety of the Grass River and miles of shoreline on Clam Lake and Lake Bellaire. The part of the natural area that is most familiar to the public, however, is south of the river. This portion of the preserve includes the Grass River Center and more than 7 miles of trails.

The Grass River is a link in Antrim County's Chain o' Lakes and connects Lake Bellaire to the smaller Clam Lake (which in turn empties into Torch Lake). The river is also fed by numerous streams and creeks, and its water is shallow and grassy—thus the name—and bordered by marshland. This makes the spot not only attractive to anglers with a yen for bass, but for bird-watchers too.

It's a fact! A chain of more than a dozen lakes connects Beals Lake to the Elk River, which empties into Grand Traverse Bay. In all, this chain of lakes spans 55 miles; the Green River Nature Area is located on this "Chain o' Lakes."

40

How Did They Get the Logs to the Mill?

Roads

Rails

Hartwick Pines State Park

DAILY, 8–10; MICHIGAN RECREATION PASSPORT REQUIRED (PAGE 7);
THE MUSEUM IS FREE
4216 Ranger Road, Grayling, MI 49738; (989) 348-2537;
www.michigan.gov/loggingmuseum

See for yourself! The park's Old Growth Forest is a 49-acre stand of virgin pine. Untouched by the lumbermen who moved through the area in the nineteenth century, the trees here are 350 to 375 years old and stand as high as 160 feet tall.

The rundown:

Hartwick Pines is a sprawling park of 9,672 acres located in the heart of Michigan, northeast of Grayling. The property includes an incredibly diverse collection of ecosystems, including everything from kettle lakes and cedar swamps to aspen stands, hardwood forest, and open grasslands. The East Branch of the Au Sable flows through the eastern corner of the park.

Most of the park's facilities are less than a mile from the main entrance. You could begin by simply driving over to the east parking lot and hopping onto the trail through the old woods, but you'd miss a bit. Instead, I recommend starting at the Hartwick Pines Visitor Center. This is where you can learn about what all those different ecosystems mean for the park—how these various habitats create a unique environment for animals and the hunters, bird-watchers, and photographers that come here.

Inside the visitor center you can explore the role of Michigan forests—exploring the past, present, and future of how timber is used and conserved. There are wildlife displays and exhibits that talk a little about the park's history. Kids and adults will get a kick out of the Talking Tree: You push a button and the large white pine talks.

From the visitor center, you will find the trail that leads back to the Logging Museum and the Old Growth Forest. The park is most famous for this stand of towering white pine. The Old Growth Forest Trail is a paved loop through the trees and is accessible to everyone. Be sure to stop along your walk to step into the idyllic Chapel in the Pines.

The Logging Museum is, appropriately enough, located inside a log building. It was constructed by the Civilian Conservation Corps during the Depression. The museum tells the story of a lumber camp. There's a cook's shanty, where meals were prepared, as well as barracks and examples of the tools they used in camp and the games they played. Throughout the summer, the museum also offers live demonstrations.

It's a fact! When the park was founded, the old-growth forest was much bigger—85 acres—but many trees were blown down by a windstorm in 1940.

41

Raven Hill Discovery Center

APR.–OCT. SUN., 2–4; MON.–FRI., 10–4; SAT., 12–4;
NOV.–MAR. SUN., 2–4; SAT., 12–4; $10
4737 Fuller Road, East Jordan, MI 49727; (231) 536-3369;
www.miravenhill.org

See for yourself! Families won't want to miss out on all the hands-on activities for kids at the Raven Hill Discovery Center—it has everything from science exhibits in the museum to a music garden and a maple-leaf-shaped tree house.

The rundown:

Located about 5 miles east of East Jordan, the Raven Hill Discovery Center is just north of the adjacent Raven Ridge Nature Preserve. The property's 157 acres include a great mix of indoor and outdoor activities as well as exhibit space. While nature is an important part of what the center is about, it's not the only thing covered here. Science, technology, history, and art are all on display and part of the experience.

You can begin your visit with the buildings. There's the Main Museum, of course, with all its hands-on activities illustrating various scientific principles. There is the Animal Room, where you can pick up and hold the various reptiles and amphibians the staff takes care of here. The Periodic Room is one of my favorites: It features a large 3-D exhibit of the periodic table, with examples of each element.

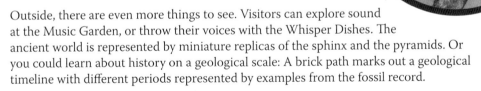

Around the grounds you will find other structures. The Energy House, for example, is a solar-powered house that illustrates what it takes to live "off the grid." The one-room schoolhouse shows a typical classroom in 1895, and the E.T. Building teaches visitors about the evolution of technology.

Outside, there are even more things to see. Visitors can explore sound at the Music Garden, or throw their voices with the Whisper Dishes. The ancient world is represented by miniature replicas of the sphinx and the pyramids. Or you could learn about history on a geological scale: A brick path marks out a geological timeline with different periods represented by examples from the fossil record.

There is plenty more to see, and if you plan ahead and come for a class or other program, the center has a fiber arts studio, a print shop, and much more. The Discovery Center has a small half-acre pond and some trails that connect up with the nearby Raven Ridge Nature Preserve, which is managed by the Little Traverse Conservancy. The preserve consists of 140 acres of woody ridges and open fields and has 1.5 miles of trail.

It's a fact! The nearby East Jordan Iron Works was founded in 1883. It originally produced casts for the timber industry, and once even made tank parts in World War II. Today it makes casts that are vital for civic infrastructure, such as valves and fire hydrants. It now owns foundries in Michigan, Oklahoma, Ireland, and France.

42

Sinkholes Pathway

DAILY, 8–10; THE MICHIGAN RECREATION PASSPORT REQUIRED (PAGE 7)
M-33 and Tomahawk Lake Highway, Onaway, MI 49765; Aloha State Park (231) 625-2522;
www.michigandnr.com/parksandtrails/details.aspx?id=52&type=SFPW

See for yourself! What happens when the bedrock consists of limestone and then it dissolves? You can see for yourself with a hike along the Sinkholes Pathway.

The rundown:

Trust me, geology can be fun, especially when you go about discovering its more interesting features on your own. The Sinkholes Pathway doesn't have a nature center. There are no specialists waiting around to tell you what you need to know. As natural attractions go, it's pretty bare bones. That's what I like about it: You find your way to the trailhead, read the signs, then go for a walk. Simple.

This part of Michigan is known for its karst topography, which exists when a porous layer of bedrock erodes, causing everything above it to sink. The bedrock in this part of northern Michigan is limestone. As you walk along the pathway, just beneath the soil under your feet is a layer of glacial till. (Glaciers scraped up a lot of sediment in their journeys south, and they dumped it willy-nilly as they retreated north.) Beneath that till is the limestone. As anyone who has visited a cave knows, limestone does not get along with water.

When it rains here, the water seeps through the till and eats away at the bedrock, and eventually that foundation layer gets too weak to support the ground above. Some of the resulting holes fill up with water (like nearby Shoepac Lake). Others continue to drain water, and life goes on as it had at the surface. After a bunch of these sinkholes form, humans sometime show up and decide to blaze a trail through the woods so everyone can get a better look.

The process takes a lot of time, and it's still going on. Two collapses in the past century have enlarged Shoepac Lake. You can see where ground has given way on the eastern side of the lake, if you know what you're looking at.

The hike takes you by five of the area's most dramatic sinkholes. It's a relatively easy 2.5-mile walk. It can be made more rigorous if you choose to hike to the bottom: The first sinkhole you come to has steps, 181 in all. Observation decks at the other holes give you a chance to appreciate the landscape. Along the way, the trail passes through thick stands of aspen and jack pine. The parking area and trailhead for the Sinkholes Pathway are just north of the Shoepac Lake campground.

It's a fact! Sinkholes can form underwater. Scientists studying sinkholes to the east under Lake Huron have discovered rare microbes that occur in only a few places on Earth.

43

WILDFLOWERS

e Swift Mammals

The Mammal Corner

We were here

The circle of life

Elizabeth Kennedy Nature Center and the Thorne Swift Nature Preserve

TRAILS APR. 15–NOV. 15, 10–SUNSET
NATURE CENTER MEMORIAL DAY–LABOR DAY DAILY, 10–7
LABOR DAY–OCT. 23, WEEKENDS ONLY
PARKING $5 FOR NON-TOWNSHIP RESIDENTS
6696 Lower Shore Drive, Harbor Springs, MI 49740; (231) 526-6401;
www.harborinc.org/thorne-swift-nature-preserve-95/

See for yourself! The Lake Michigan Overlook is a wooden platform on a protected stretch of dunes. You can't walk down to the water here, but the view is amazing.

The rundown:

Located 4 miles west of Harbor Springs and overlooking Lake Michigan, the Thorne Swift Nature Preserve consists of 30 acres of upland dunes, cedar swamp, and 950 feet of Lake Michigan shoreline.

From the trailhead near the Elizabeth Kennedy Nature Center, the preserve's two main trails head off in opposite directions, meeting together closer to the beach, like the two sides of a bow. The Cedar Trail heads off to the right and curves through a cedar swamp. The Balsam Trail heads to the left and brings you through a large stand of white and yellow birch. In essence they make up one long loop, and they're joined by a third trail that makes a beeline to the water and the preserve's 300 feet of shoreline.

In the summer, naturalists give guided walks through the preserve. There's even a nighttime walk that takes advantage of the region's incredibly clear skies and almost no light pollution.

None of these trails are all that long—all together they add up to 1.5 miles—but that's not to say they're not worth walking. Cedar swamps along Lake Michigan are some of the state's most beautiful natural spaces. Along the path you will also find interpretive signage, a platform overlooking the property's small pond, a woodland gazebo, and an amphitheater.

Very little of the space in the cedar-paneled nature center is unused. There are birds and animal skins mounted on the walls and a touch table with turtle shells, antlers, and turkey feathers. Different activities are scheduled throughout the summer, and in the spring and fall, the nature center hosts many schoolchildren.

It's a fact! A bent tree once leaned out from a steep bluff over Lake Michigan near here. It was apparently notable enough to inspire the Odawa to call the region "it is bent" or *Waganakising*. The French translated that to *L'Arbre Croche*, and the English went and called the place the Land of the Crooked Tree.

Northern Upper Peninsula

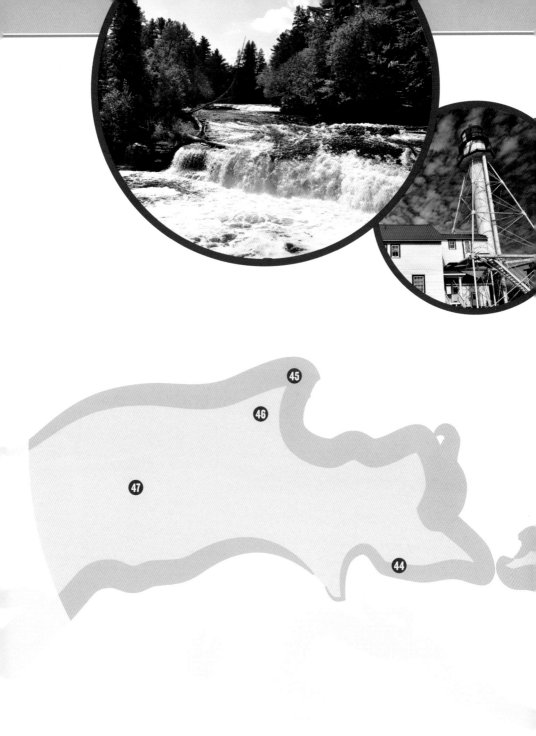

44

Marquette Island Preserves

OPEN YEAR-ROUND; FREE
Marquette Island, Cedarville, MI 49719; (231) 347-0991
www.landtrust.org

See for yourself! The area is a bird-watching paradise during the spring migration. The North Huron Birding Trail passes through the area. The website www.northhuronbirding.com will help you find the best time to go birding on Marquette Island.

The rundown:

Les Cheneaux is a region of 36 islands and channels nestled along the northern shore of Lake Huron, east of Mackinac Island. Les Cheneaux is French for "the channels" and describes the area quite well. The towns of Hessel and Cedarville are situated on the mainland, just behind the islands, which in turn provide the towns with some protection from weather on the lake. French voyageurs, who first gave the place its current name, sheltered from storms on these islands when in need.

The Little Traverse Conservancy manages three nature preserves on Marquette Island, the largest of these islands. The preserves are named Leopold, Seiberling-Stewart, and Sheppard-Hardy. Together they add up to more than 1,500 acres of protected land.

Getting to the island is the first hurdle for visitors. According to the conservancy, the beach in Hessel has a public put-in for paddlers. It's about a 2-mile paddle from the beach in Hessel to the trailhead on Marquette Island that leads into the Aldo Leopold Preserve. Woods & Water Ecotours & Adventure Gear in Hessel rent kayaks and canoes. If paddling isn't your thing, Hills Point Resort in Cedarville rents motorboats and can point you in the right direction. Of course, if you visit in the winter and the lake is frozen over, you can walk across to the island.

In the past, the trails through the preserves were a bit haphazard. In recent years, volunteers have been out doing trail maintenance and installing some signage. Accordingly, there should be trail maps at most intersections on the preserve. The island is covered in a thick conifer forest. There are few beaches, and in recent years, the shoreline has been getting more and more marshy. (If water levels continue to rise, however, that might change.) Be sure to stay on the trails and avoid private property, as much of the island is privately owned. Most of the trails end up taking you back to the water. The preserves account for about 5 miles of lake frontage, so an interesting trip might be to paddle or motor around the island, find preserve trails, and explore them with short excursions into the woods.

It's a fact! The Aldo Leopold Preserve is named for the famous forester, conservationist, and author *(The Sand County Almanac)*. As a boy, Leopold spent his summers at his family's cottage on Marquette Island.

45

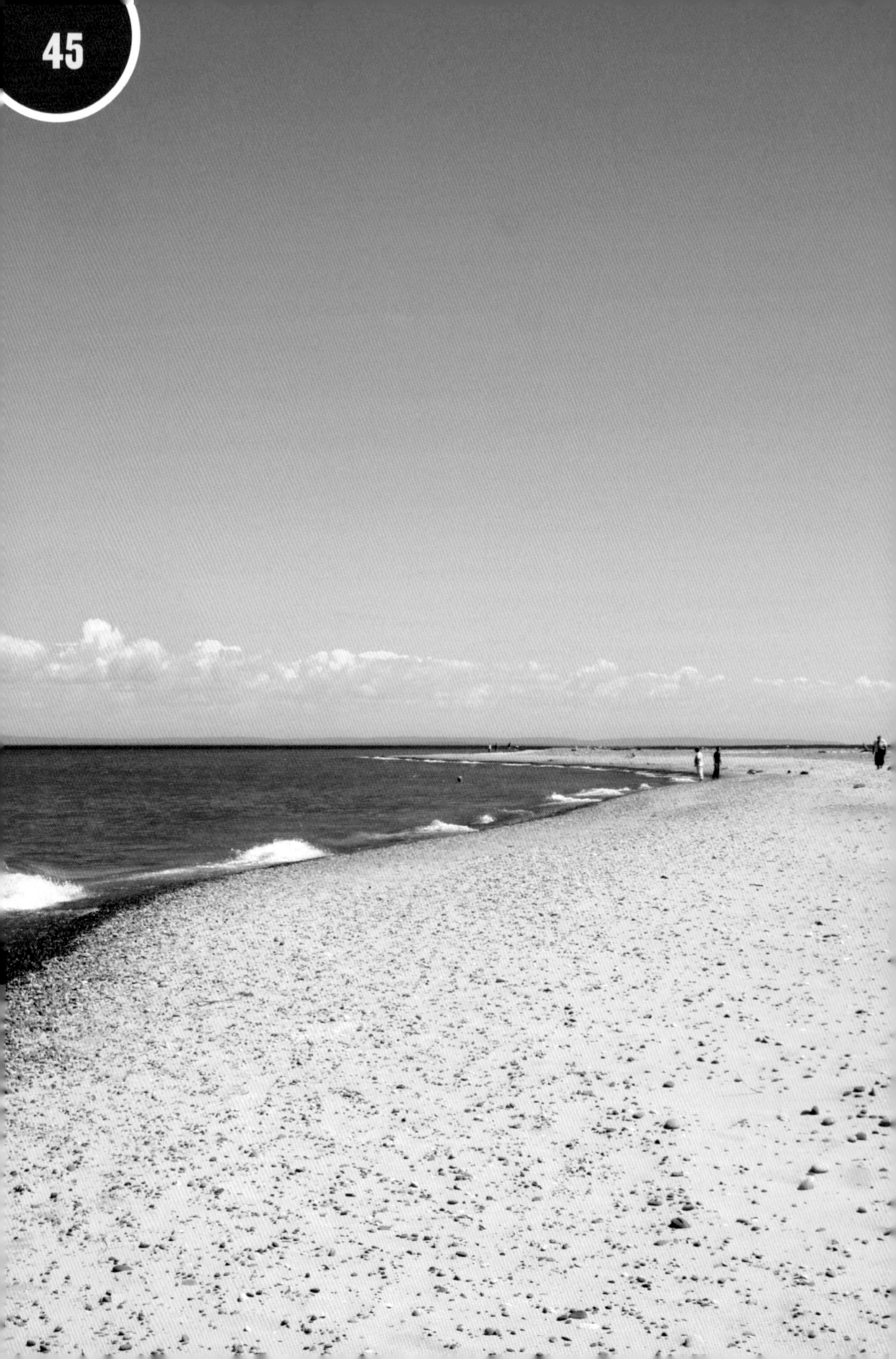

Whitefish Point Bird Observatory

OPEN YEAR-ROUND, DAWN TO DUSK; FREE
16914 North Whitefish Point Road, Paradise, MI 49768; (906) 492-3596;
www.wpbo.org

See for yourself! Whitefish Point Bird Observatory holds bird counts several times a year—for waterbirds in spring and fall and for hawks in the spring. During these counts, the hawk deck and water bird shack are open to visitors. For nature lovers who enjoy experiencing the elements, these are great times to visit and to make a contribution to science!

The rundown:

The tourists who flock to Whitefish Point to visit the famous lighthouse and museum or to stand on the beach and look out over that stretch of Lake Superior known as the "Graveyard of the Great Lakes" might be forgiven for overlooking the point's feathery visitors. Every year, Whitefish Point attracts tens of thousands of migrating birds in the spring and fall, which is why the Whitefish Point Bird Observatory was established.

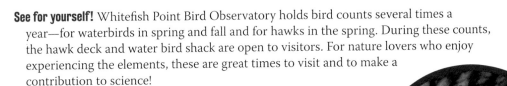

The first birds heading north in the spring are the owls and hawks, followed by waterbirds. These are the populations the observatory staff tracks regularly with scheduled counts, but the flow of birds doesn't end with the coming of summer. In fact, by the end of July some birds are already heading back south. An observation guide on the observatory's website will give you a good idea of what to look for when you visit.

In terms of facilities, the observatory has a small footprint: It's home to one building, which is located across the parking lot from the lighthouse and holds the Owl's Roost Gift Shop and a small classroom. There is also a banding lab inside, where staff members band owls.

While I get a kick out of visiting in the "off season," most people visiting Whitefish Point come in the summer to see the Shipwreck Museum or the lighthouse, or they're camping at nearby Tahquamenon Falls and looking for a diversion for the day. A visit to the bird observatory will be more rewarding if you intentionally include it in your plans and come prepared. Bring binoculars, consult a field guide beforehand, and plan for the weather. That latter bit is especially important. If you're not from the Upper Peninsula, you might be surprised how cold it can be on Whitefish Point, even in summer. When the wind comes in from across the water, it's downright chilly, so pack accordingly.

It's a fact! Nearly 350 bird species have been seen at Whitefish Point, and they've included everything from loons and jaegers to owls, woodpeckers, and raptors. They've even spotted more than 30 species of warblers and northern finches here!

46

Tahquamenon Falls State Park

OPEN YEAR-ROUND, 8–10;
THE MICHIGAN RECREATION PASSPORT IS REQUIRED (PAGE 7)
41382 West M-123, Paradise, MI 49768; (906) 492-3415;
www.michigan.gov/tahquamenonfalls

See for yourself! The Upper Brink Stairway takes you down to the very edge of Tahquamenon Falls, and the observation deck is perfect for pictures.

The rundown:

The Upper Peninsula has a wealth of waterfalls. Most of these occur in the western two thirds of the peninsula, where rivers descend rapidly to Lake Superior. Many folks will tell you that Bond Falls, north of Watersmeet, is the most beautiful waterfall in Michigan, but the most impressive by sheer volume and scope is found farther east.

Tahquamenon Falls drops 50 feet into the Tahquamenon River, and its crest spans 200 feet between the forested edges of the river. This makes Tahquamenon the second largest falls east of the Mississippi, a position that inevitably leads to many comparisons with Niagara Falls, which occupies the top spot. Though you might see a resemblance between the two—especially when Niagara is viewed from the Canadian side—Tahquamenon stands up just fine on its own. Though two-thirds smaller than Niagara, Tahquamenon Falls is beautiful, impressive, and has been drawing satisfied visitors for generations.

I am speaking, of course, of Upper Tahquamenon Falls. This is the park's main attraction. About 4 miles downstream, however, you'll find the Lower Tahquamenon Falls. These falls are less dramatic and much shorter, but they're inviting for another reason—they're a popular swimming and wading location, as you can walk right out into cedar-steeped waters of the river.

Visitors to the state park almost always visit to see the falls, but many overlook everything else the park has to offer. Throughout the summer, the day-use parking lot is full of cars, RVs, and camper trailers. The real nature lovers, however, will look beyond the geology that created the stunning waterfall to the ecology that surrounds them. The park features two campgrounds, as well as some incredible hiking opportunities. You can walk from the Upper Falls down to the mouth of the river on Lake Superior—a route that overlaps a portion of the North Country Trail—or take on one of the loops that lead back to the lakes north of M-123. Be on the lookout for wildlife too. The last time we visited Tahquamenon Falls, a black bear lurched across the road in front of our car, soon lost in a clamor of twigs and leaves; the area's many moose are also often spotted by visitors.

It's a fact! When the river's water levels are at their highest, 50,000 gallons of water pour over Tahquamenon Falls every second.

47

Seney National Wildlife Refuge

OPEN YEAR-ROUND DURING DAYLIGHT HOURS; FREE
1674 Refuge Entrance Road, Seney, MI 49883; (906) 586-9851;
www.fws.gov/refuge/seney/

See for yourself! You can see the wetlands up close with a hike or see the sights from your car by driving the 7-mile Marshland Wildlife Drive.

The rundown:

After the lumber companies passed through this part of the Upper Peninsula, there was an attempt to make the land viable for agriculture. The original owners of this land hoped to make something of the property by draining the wetlands and selling parcels to farmers. The enterprise failed—the land simply wasn't good for growing crops—and in 1935, the Seney National Wildlife Refuge was established. The job of creating a refuge for the region's migratory birds and local wildlife fell to the Civilian Conservation Corps (CCC) and the Work Projects Administration. They erected dikes, dug canals, and created a system that impounded over 7,000 acres of open water. Today, the refuge covers more than 95,000 acres. The western portion of the property includes the 25,000-acre Seney Wilderness Area, which in turn includes the 10,000-acre Strangmoor Bog National Natural Landmark.

That's a lot of property, and it can be a bit overwhelming to contemplate. Fortunately, our destination keeps us in the eastern part of the refuge where we find the Visitor Center, nature trails, and the Marshland Wildlife Drive. The Visitor Center includes a small exhibit space, a gift shop/bookstore, and an information desk. There's a large touch table in the middle of the room where kids can pet a stuffed goose, pick up turtle shells, and examine various animal skulls.

The nature trails all begin at the Visitor Center. The short Pine Ridge Trail is only 1.4 miles long, but there are other options if you want a more extensive hike. Back in the day, the CCC built a unique rest stop on M-77 called the Wigwams because it consisted of two large cone-shaped buildings connected by a roof. This picnic area fell into disrepair over time, but within the last 10 years, it has been restored. You can get there by way of a short connector path off the Pine Ridge Trail.

Seney's many loons, bald eagles, sandhill cranes, and trumpeter swans (not to mention beaver and otters) are drawn here because of the many ponds and pools. The Marshland Wildlife Drive is a 7-mile, one-way road through marsh and forest with three observation decks. The road winds around five ponds, and you might be amazed at how much wildlife you can spot from a car, so bring a camera.

It's a fact! Today, there are around 5 million Canada geese in North America, but when the Seney National Wildlife Refuge was established in 1935, they were a threatened species.

Western Upper Peninsula

48

MooseWood Nature Center

OPEN YEAR-ROUND ON WEEKENDS, 12–4; FREE
2 Peter White Drive, Marquette, MI 49855 (Presque Isle Park); (906) 228-6250
www.moosewood.org

See for yourself! Located in Presque Isle Park, visitors can follow Peter White Drive around for scenic views of the rocky cliffs overlooking Lake Superior.

The rundown:

MooseWood is a relatively new addition to Michigan's network of nature centers. The organization was founded a little more than 20 years ago with the idea that Marquette needed a nature center. The center is now located near the entrance to Presque Isle Park in the building that once held the Shiras Pool, a local swimming hole.

The Shiras Pool itself has become one of the center's big projects. Once a thriving wetland, the pool was dredged in the early twentieth century to make a swimming pond. Geese and other waterfowl flocked to the pool, and folks grew wary of the water quality. Eventually, the whole thing was pumped out and lined with concrete. Maintenance on a pool that's 37,000 square feet isn't cheap or easy, and by 2006, the pool was closed. The MooseWood Nature Center is leading the charge to reverse the changes to the natural area here by turning the pool back into a vibrant wetland habitat.

The building that once saw hundreds of summer bathers is now the nature center. There are interpretive displays, a small collection of live animals, and information on the region's natural history. The center is open only on weekends, but the staff is out in the community working with local schools to help the next generation learn to protect the environment.

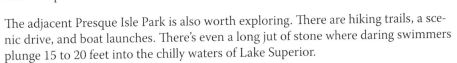

In addition to the work with schools, MooseWood offers a host of programs and activities. There's one for junior naturalists and another for bird lovers. One of the center's regular programs is also one of its most popular—the guided Bog Walk Tour is worth a trip to the center all by itself. Be sure to check out the site for more information on that unique nature experience.

The adjacent Presque Isle Park is also worth exploring. There are hiking trails, a scenic drive, and boat launches. There's even a long jut of stone where daring swimmers plunge 15 to 20 feet into the chilly waters of Lake Superior.

It's a fact! There are a number of places named Presque Isle in Michigan; the name is French and means "almost an island" and refers to a peninsula that is just barely connected to the mainland.

49

Echo Lake Nature Preserve

OPEN YEAR-ROUND, DAWN TO DUSK; FREE
Big Bay Road, Negaunee, MI 49866; Nature Conservancy (U.P. Office) (906) 225-0399
www.nature.org/ourinitiatives/regions/northamerica/unitedstates/michigan/placesweprotect/
echo-lake-nature-preserve.xml

See for yourself! From the treeless granite overlook above Echo Lake, you get a great view of Lake Superior. From that height you can see nearby Presque Isle, Granite Island, and Hogback Mountain in the distance.

The rundown:

Just a 10-minute drive west of Marquette, the Echo Lake Nature Preserve features some of the region's most attractive scenery. A 20-acre lake is bordered on one side by high stone cliffs. Surrounded by forest and cut through by Harlow Creek, the preserve is a fine place for a hike, picnic, or simply a warm swim (at least, warmer than in Lake Superior).

To get there, take Big Bay Road north. About 7.5 miles after crossing the Dead River leaving town, you will see the entrance for the preserve on your left. About 1.7 miles in, park the car and hike the last half mile to the lake. There are two trails here. One leads out to the small peninsula. The other leads to the granite perch overlooking the lake and surrounding area.

The hardwood forests around the lower parts of the lake are primarily populated with sugar maple. Where the bedrock is closer to the surface, the character of the forest changes to one of predominantly paper birch and red oak.

Usually a preserve like this doesn't have much in the way of facilities and staff. However, there is a full-time intern in the summer who leads nature hikes and offers some interpretive programs.

Though the lake is at the heart of the preserve, the entire conservation easement is a whopping 480 acres. About 25 percent of that is bare rock that's sparsely covered with stunted species of pine and oak. The conservancy notes that several rare Michigan species grow here, including pine-drops, dwarf bilberry, and big-leaf sandwort. The property also has large stands of large northern white cedar and its grove of eastern hemlock.

Echo Lake is a headwater lake; Harlow Creek flows out of the lake and down to Lake Superior. Echo Lake is also very deep, measuring 70 feet at its greatest depth.

It's a fact! Stands of eastern hemlock are important for large mammals. An exceptionally large and dense stand of eastern hemlock here helps protect moose and deer from the region's hard winters.

119

50

Sylvania Wilderness and Recreation Area

ENTRANCE STATION OPEN SAT.–THU., 8:30–5; FRI., 8:30–6
VEHICLE PASS $5 (DAY), $20 (SEASON)
Thousand Island Lake Road, Watersmeet, MI 49969
(906) 358-4724; Ottawa National Forest, (906) 932-1330
www.fs.usda.gov/recarea/ottawa/recarea/?recid=12331

See for yourself! If you have never gone canoe camping, Sylvania Wilderness is a great place for your first trip.

The rundown:
In 1895 a Wisconsin lumberman, A. D. Johnston, bought 80 acres of forest on the north shore of Clark Lake. When he visited the spot, he became enamored and decided to make the spot a summer retreat. Soon he was inviting his wealthy friends to buy property and join him in the pristine North Woods. Together they created the Sylvania Club, which eventually became the heart of the Sylvania Wilderness.

Today, Sylvania has grown to more than 18,000 acres, and that can be a little overwhelming. There are several ways to tackle this wilderness and experience its natural charms. The first is to take advantage of the day-use areas. The most popular is Clark Lake, but there is easy access to many other lakes in the area. All of these are perfect for a short paddle. Stop by, put a boat in the water, and start exploring.

Another option is to stay a few days. You can do that at the campground at the north end of Clark Lake. The campground has decent facilities—flush toilets and running water—but for showers you will have to walk or drive down to the day-use area where there is a large comfort station. Camping at Sylvania gives you a chance to spend a couple of days paddling around the local lakes.

To really experience Sylvania, however, put that boat in the water, load it up with your camping gear, and head out into the wild. There are campsites scattered throughout Sylvania on lakes big and small. (In all, there are 34 named lakes in the area.) Some spots might require portaging (carrying your canoe), but not all do. Many of these wilderness campsites are also accessible via hiking trails. So if backpacking is your thing, you can forgo the water and walk to your site.

It's a fact! The Sylvania Wilderness sits on some of the highest ground in the Midwest. Its waters are kept clean by the fact that no streams feed the rivers and lakes here; springs and rainfall feed them; water flows out from Sylvania rather than into the wilderness.

51

Kitch-iti-kipi at Palms Book State Park

OPEN YEAR-ROUND;
THE MICHIGAN RECREATION PASSPORT IS REQUIRED (PAGE 7)
Manistique, MI 49854 (located at northern end of M-149, north off US 2); (906) 341-2355;
www.michigan.gov/palmsbook

See for yourself! To see the Big Spring up close, visitors climb aboard an observation raft and then pull themselves—by way of a cable and a large wheel—out to the middle of the spring.

The rundown:

For what has been described as a "major U.P. tourist attraction," Palm Book State Park is very low key. The big attraction here for day-trippers is the Big Spring, otherwise known as Kitch-iti-kipi. Since I pronounce it wrong every time, I usually call it "that clear spring near Manistique, you know, the really deep one with the raft." And that's essentially what it is: a big clear spring with a raft. But that description undersells its many charms.

Located west of Manistique on the northwestern side of Indian Lake, Kitch-iti-kipi is a large pool fed by an underwater spring. The pool feeds a small creek that empties into nearby Indian Lake, which in turn empties into the Indian and Manistique Rivers and eventually into Lake Michigan. A lot of water is rushing out from the spring, but all that potential for turbulence stays well below the surface. Instead, at Palm Book State Park you'll find a quiet woodland pond surrounded by cedar forest. The pool itself is a large oval, about 250 feet across at its widest point. A cable is strung across the pool, west-to-east; a large observation raft is docked on the spring's west side. The center of the raft features a viewing port that enables you to peer straight down, and the water itself is unbelievably clear. From the surface you can see down 40 feet. It is so clear that the rocks and fallen logs on the bottom look close enough to touch. You get a sense of the depth only when you see how small the shadow cast by the raft is. Look closer and you can see sand moving in the current, and you'll see large trout swim idly by, unbothered by the audience. Because it's spring-fed, the water is a constant 45 degrees year-round. This makes it too cold for swimming in summer, and it also means that it never freezes over in winter. Snowmobilers often make treks out to the spring when it is surrounded by snow.

While at the park, be sure to look into some of the history. The spring was once treated as a dump site by the lumbering industry, and it was preserved thanks to the efforts of Jim Bellaire, who helped secure the property for public enjoyment. There is a lot of alleged American Indian lore surrounding Kitch-iti-tipi, but don't believe everything you hear. The most reliable legend is that Bellaire, the owner of a small business who helped draw attention to the site, once thought the spring needed a quaint tale or two to attract visitors.

It's a fact! The spring kicks out more than 10,000 gallons of water a minute.

52

Black River Scenic Byway Waterfalls

OPEN YEAR-ROUND; FREE
Black River Road, Bessemer, MI 49911 (north from Bessemer to Lake Superior);
Bessemer Ranger District of the Ottawa National Forest: (906) 932-1330;
www.fs.usda.gov/recarea/ottawa/recarea/?recid=12343

See for yourself! The Black River crashes through five stunning waterfalls on its steep descent to Lake Superior.

The rundown:

The upper stretch of the Black River gives no hint to the turmoil that awaits downstream. For many, the Black River is a great body of water for a quiet canoe trip or some fishing. The lower section of the river is something else altogether.

The waterfalls begin close to the Copper Peak ski jump; there you'll find the Narrows, Chippewa Falls, and Algonquin Falls. These are the river's smallest drops and have limited access. The Black River Scenic Byway officially begins with Great Conglomerate Falls. It's a short hike—less than a mile—to the river from the parking area. The river drops 30 feet here, and at the top of the waterfall, it is split by a large conglomerate rock.

Less than a mile north of that first parking area, you come to the trailhead parking area for Potawatomi and Gorge Falls. The falls are close to each other—just 900 feet separates them, and a short hike on the paved trail brings you to an observation point. Because the site has bathrooms and is accessible to those with disabilities, it's very popular with travelers. At the Potawatomi Falls, the river drops about 40 feet. The river then narrows considerably and drops another 20 feet, creating Gorge Falls.

If you head north on the scenic byway another 0.7 mile, you'll come to the parking area for Sandstone Falls. From here, it's a short walk (0.25 mile) to the falls, which are less dramatic than those mentioned above. The river makes two drops here, for a combined fall of 25 feet.

Rainbow Falls is the last waterfall on this tour, and it's located near the end of the scenic byway where it empties into Black River National Harbor. It may be the most dramatic of the bunch. The hike back to the falls would be an easy half mile if it weren't for the climb. Visitors have to huff up and down 200 steps to see the 45-foot drop, but it's worth it.

It's a fact! The Black River gets its name from the dark hue of its waters. It gets this coloration from tannins, naturally produced dyes found in tree bark, especially area hemlock trees.

53

Nara Nature Park and Nara Chalet Interpretive Center

CHALET OPEN DAILY, 8–8; FREE
616 Shelden Avenue, Houghton, MI 49931; (906) 482-1700
www.naranaturepark.com

See for yourself! A walk is often better with a friend. If you're traveling solo and want some companionship, you can stop by the Copper Country Humane Society shelter at the Nara Nature Park and volunteer to walk one of their canine guests.

The rundown:

The Nara Nature Park is just 2 miles east of Houghton on the other side of Michigan Tech University. Overlooking the south shore of Portage Lake, the park's 100 acres include the mouth of the Pilgrim River and are connected to the sprawling Michigan Tech trail system. The park began nearly two decades ago when Bob and Ruth Nara donated property to the city for the Nara Nature Trail. Over time, property was added to connect up with the Michigan Tech property, and more trails were blazed. In 2005, the building for the Copper Country Humane Society was completed, and a couple of years after that, the Nara Nature Chalet was open to the public. The chalet is unique in its purpose. Though it does have some interpretive information, the real attractions are the hot showers, fireplace, and restrooms. This is cross-country territory, and there's nothing better than being able to warm up, shower, and get into warm, dry clothes after a long, good ski. And if long trips are your thing—be it in the snow, on a bike, or in your tennis shoes—Nara is the place to start.

Several of the trails begin on the east side of US 41; this is where you'll find the Nara Nature Park Boardwalks. These are two elevated boardwalks that run down both sides of Pilgrim River, on its north and south banks. The other is the Peepsock Trail, which follows Peepsock Creek down to Portage Lake. The trailhead for the other group of trails is next to the chalet. There are a few different loops, but things start to get interesting once you discover the connector trails to the Michigan Tech trail system. Combined, these two properties offer 50 miles of trail for hiking, biking, snowshoeing, and cross-country skiing. Not all trails are open for all activities, so visitors need to familiarize themselves with the trails before heading out.

One activity that visitors enjoy is stopping by the animal shelter to pick up a dog. You don't have to commit to a lifetime, but the animals certainly get a lot out of the exercise and the companionship.

It's a fact! Nearby Michigan Tech uses the Nara Nature Park for its biology, geology, and forestry classes.

54

Estivant Pines Wilderness Nature Sanctuary

OPEN DAILY, DAWN TO DUSK; FREE
Burma Road, Copper Harbor, MI 49918; Michigan Nature Association, (866) 223-2231
www.michigannature.org/home/sancts/estivant/estivant.shtml

See for yourself! The white pine is Michigan's state tree. This is the only place in the Upper Peninsula where you can walk beneath a virgin stand of white pine; the trees here are up to 150 feet tall.

The rundown:

There are very few places in the Midwest that were untouched by the lumberman's ax. Millions of acres of forest were stripped, and millions upon millions of trees were sent down rivers to faraway mills. These woody giants fed steamships, built the railroad, and provided the material for everything from books to furniture.

The original forest that blanketed this part of the country is unimaginable to the people who live and play here today, but there are virgin stands of trees left. In Hartwick Pines State Park, there is the Old Growth Forest. Here on the Keweenaw Peninsula, just south of Copper Harbor, is another. The Estivant Pines Wilderness Nature Sanctuary is a 508-acre preserve of old-growth eastern white pine. The property is maintained by the Michigan Nature Association, and there are no facilities; the forest and wilderness are the sole attractions.

The main trail through the property is the Memorial Grove Trail. It's a 1.2-mile hike. Connected to this is the Cathedral Loop Trail, which is about a mile in length. Each can be walked as a "lollipop loop" (a loop with a short handle out to the trailhead), or you can stitch them together for a longer walk.

There's a third trail, but it requires old-fashioned U.P. grit. The Fallen Giant Trail leads out from the southern junction of the other two. At the trailhead is a sign, which even Dante couldn't have improved on: THIS UNMAINTAINED TRAIL CROSSES A SWAMP AND A RIVER. RECOMMENDED ONLY FOR EXPERIENCED HIKERS WITH PROPER GEAR. Those who've made the trek tell me it's worth it.

Another thing of note: Mosquitoes are no joke here. I was at a store on the Keweenaw buying bug repellent, and a couple next to me was also buying bug spray. As the husband reached for some brand with 10 or 15 percent DEET, his wife stopped him and said, "Put that back. They carry that stuff for the tourists." I took the hint: It's not always fly or skeeter season here, but when it is, you have to be prepared and buy the heavy-duty stuff (25 to 40 percent).

It's a fact! In 1668, when French missionaries founded the first mission over in Sault Ste. Marie, many of the white pines here were already well more than 150 years old.

The Michigan Nature Explorer's Adventure Pack

Experiencing a nature center or nature preserve requires very little preparation. Except for sites that require some hiking—in which case you need good shoes, a bottle of water, and an awareness of the weather—just stopping by is always okay. With a little planning, however, you can get more out of your visit.

Here are some suggestions for things you might want to include in an "adventure pack." Kids love having their own bags, and the experience of deciding what to bring builds their excitement.

Keeping a Record

The experts tell us that we remember more when we write stuff down by hand. Taking time to keep a record of your observations is an excellent way to engage with nature. You don't have to be an eloquent writer or an accomplished sketch artist to jot down or draw what you see around you. I have also found that carrying a camera on my walks helps me see things in a different light.

Notebook: You can find notebooks everywhere. If you're serious about the task, however, look for a waterproof notebook, which is perfect for jotting down observations in the rain.

Writing, drawing, or painting tools: Choose whatever works best: pens, pencils, colored pencils, markers, watercolors, etc.

Digital camera: A smartphone camera is often enough, but a high-quality digital camera can do so much more.

Taking a Closer Look

If you have a favorite nature center nearby, it might begin to grow too familiar. That's when you need a different perspective. Bird-watchers know the importance of a good pair of binoculars, but even a cheaper set will give you a chance to see things not readily visible. A magnifying glass, on the other hand, can reveal how much life teems in every square foot.

Binoculars: Binoculars run the gamut when it comes to price and craftmanship; even a moderately priced pair can last years. A monocular is another option.

Magnifying glass: In place of the ubiquitous Sherlock Holmes lollipop magnifying glass, many people bring a hand-held magnifier that folds up and fits in a pocket.

Learning More

The best resources for learning about a site are often the interpretive signs or brochures provided by the nature centers themselves. Sometimes it helps to set a goal for your visit. Maybe you want to learn to identify Michigan trees or wildflowers or birds. You can learn about these things in a guidebook—and there are many—but you learn so much more on the ground, so to speak. Also, not all of the guides are paperbound these days. There are some great apps for identifying leaves or bird calls.

Guidebooks: See the *Recommended Reading* list on page 132 for the guidebooks that I count on.

Smartphone with apps: There are three apps that I go to all the time: *Audubon Birds and Butterflies*, which has descriptions and samples of bird calls; *Leafsnap*, which helps you identify trees; and *Pocket Universe*, which enables you to identify nearly every feature of the night sky. Note: All of the above are iPhone apps, but comparable apps exist on other platforms.

Staying Safe and Warm

It's a shame that most folks only go outside when the weather is ideal. As a kid, our scout camp had an excellent nature hike that included a boardwalk that passed through a large wetland. We were challenged to experience the trail during each of the four seasons. In the spring, the water was high and the trail muddy. The boards bounced under our feet and dipped into the water. In the summer, there were bugs everywhere, and we looked forward to getting back under the shade of the woods. Fall came and turned the wetlands from green to tan, and the cattails broke apart in cottony puffs. And when snow finally came, there were no leaves to block the chilly wind that blew across the frozen ground. It would be a shame to miss out on all of that because we were waiting for ideal conditions. Be sure to bring the following along:

Water bottle
Granola bars
Wide-brimmed hat
Raincoat or poncho
Safety whistle

Miscellaneous

GPS unit for geocaching
Compass
Map of preserve or nature center
Swiss Army knife

The Michigan Nature Explorer's Reading List

Several years ago I went on a spring ephemeral wildflower hike with a local expert on wildflowers. The group I was with quizzed her relentlessly about every flicker of color we saw pushing up through the dead leaves of the forest. With forty-some odd years of doing this, she knew a lot. When asked how she remembered it all, she told us it was all due to going out and looking up flowers. She admitted that if she skips one spring of guiding walks, she forgets half of what she knew the year before.

Most people probably don't have time to become experts on wildflowers or trees or birds, but we still want to know what we're looking at. Thankfully, experts write guides. Here is a list of guides that sit on my shelf that have proven pretty useful. Most speak for themselves, but I offer some commentary on a handful.

General Regional Guides

Michigan Roadside Naturalist by J. Alan Holman and Margaret B. Holman. University of Michigan Press, 2003.

> This is a fun book to take on a road trip through Michigan. The authors point out numerous natural features of the state—from rare stands of trees to unique geology.

A Field Guide to the Natural Communities of Michigan by Joshua G. Cohen, Michael A. Kost, Bradford S. Slaughter, and Dennis A. Albert, Michigan State University Press, 2014.

> This one might be a bit technical for some readers—I thought so, at times—but it's very helpful in explaining the complex relationships that define the state's different natural communities.

Atlas of Early Michigan's Forests, Grasslands, and Wetlands by Dennis A. Albert and Patrick J. Comer, Michigan State University Press, 2018.

> This unique atlas compiles survey information from the nineteenth century and gives readers a chance to see the ecology of an area as it was 150 to 200 years ago.

Guides to Flora

Tree Finder: A Manual for Identification of Trees by their Leaves (Eastern US) by May Theilgaard Watts. Nature Study Guild Publishers, 1991.

> This short guide to identifying trees has been around for 25 years. By following the key, you will be able to identify most trees in the woods. Watts also wrote *Winter Tree Finder: A Manual for Identifying Deciduous Trees in Winter (Eastern US)*— if your explorations don't end when the snow starts falling.

Trees of Michigan by Stan Tekiela, Adventure Publications, 2002.

> Like the following book on wildflowers, this is a great guide to toss in a backpack. It's small, concise, and filled with information.

Wildflowers of Michigan Field Guide by Stan Tekiela, Adventure Publications, 2000.

Michigan Trees & Wildflowers: A Folding Pocket Guide to Familiar Species, Waterford Press, 2004.

Guides to Fauna

BIRDS

Wild About Michigan Birds: A Youth's Guide to the Birds of Michigan by Adele Porter, Adventure Publications, 2009.

> Some guides might seem dull to kids. This one is a great introduction for the younger nature explorers in your family.

Midwestern Birds: Backyard Guide by Bill Thompson, Cool Springs Press, 2013.

Michigan Birds: A Folding Pocket Guide to Familiar Species, Waterford Press, 2001.

ANIMALS

Critters of Michigan Pocket Guide, Adventure Publications, 2000.

Michigan Wildlife: A Folding Pocket Guide to Familiar Species, Waterford Press, 2005.

About the Author

A native of Michigan, Matt Forster has lived in the Midwest, New England, and the Rocky Mountain regions of the country. This experience has contributed much the books he's written so far—*Best Tent Camping: Michigan, Backroads & Byways of Michigan, Best Hikes Near Detroit and Ann Arbor, Backroads & Byways of Ohio, and Explorer's Guide Colorado.* When he explores Michigan, he travels with his wife and their two children. This has created some great opportunities to learn how to best camp, hike, and discover nature with kids. The family currently lives in a restored nineteenth-century schoolhouse on a small lot that backs up to one of Oakland County's largest parks, with a fine nature center just 520 yards (as the heron flies) from his desk.

Notes

Notes